ECONOMIC EUDAIMONISM

ECONOMIC EUDAIMONISM

... A CULTURAL AWAKENING

RAYMOND CHLADNY

MILL CITY PRESS

Mill City Press, Inc.
2301 Lucien Way #415
Maitland, FL 32751
407.339.4217
www.millcitypress.net

Library of Congress Control Number: 2022914235

Paperback ISBN-13: 978-1-6628-5518-4
Ebook ISBN-13: 978-1-6628-5519-1

Cover Picture:

A sunset or sunrise? It's totally up to each of us through our personal choices of economic purpose, fulfillment, and happiness. There are two main sources, known as hedonic and eudaimonic. Hedonic, from which the word hedonism originates, is self-pleasure in all things. Eudaimonism seeks happiness through meaning and purpose, requiring it to be ethically grounded. Most of the economic philosophers stressed the importance of ethics with our business dealings, yet today we see such extremes between poverty and wealth, the likes of which these economic founders could have never imagined . . . disparities so large that they are undermining our faith in a free market system, leading to a growing push for increased government regulation and socialism to counter these self-indulgences. This current path has forgotten the destructive history born from restricted freedoms. Only through the light of logic and disclosure can we find a safe haven, an amazing, vibrant cultural awakening of higher meaning and purpose.

Preface

Economics is the life blood of every civilization, and depending on its inner workings, it can enslave or free us. When allowed to work properly, it will enrich and expand the human experience for all people and our physical world . . . Economic Eudaimonism ("you-die-mon-ism").

To many, the free market, epitomized by capitalism, conjures images of stripped forests, polluted waters, smoke stacks, and toiling laborers in sweat shops while the perpetrators live in mansions adorned with large yachts and private jets.

To the contrary, this book will demonstrate historically, logically, and graphically that a capitalist free market, by its very nature, holds the greatest potential for a future of ethical and sustainable economics we know.

If you find this statement repugnant, then you are the person this book is most intended.

We all see the ugly part of our economic world with many leaders of industry and government following deep-rooted choices of power and greed with unlimited personal profits. This lack of ethics toward themselves, the planet, and our technology all lead toward instability. Kin to this narcissism is the belief of being superior based on wealth or power; an arrogant mental attitude, and as an accepted norm, could be far more dangerous than our current environmental threats (see Ethical Treatment toward Service). These changes are free and simple to make, embracing morality and respect; a healthier cultural mindset, one organic in nature.

The concept of ethics and economics is not a new one, with ethical references found in the Old Testament (1200–165 BC). It references stories of Joseph and Solomon, where economic cooperation and exchange toward an early framework of free market exchange for the public's wellbeing was being practiced.

Based on; Sigmund Wagner-Tsukamoto, *Ethical Principles of Old Testament Economics: Implications for the Teaching of Business Ethic* (University of Leicester, 1-30-2015), Vol. 3 Article 16.

Later, Aristotle (384–322 BC) in his Nicomachean Ethics, listed many virtues including justice "*The 'equality' part has to do with not grasping for more than what is fair. The just person wants their fair share, not more, not less.*" providing a just foundation for an open free market.

Source, The University of Vermont, https://www.uvm.edu/~jbailly/courses/clas158/notes/kraut4.html, extracted July, 01, 2021.

Modern economic founding fathers taught that any fully living society's economics must include virtues. Adam Smith wrote about the importance of the free market and its checks and balances provided by an invisible hand. He argued that prudence, justice, and benevolence are essential for it all to work. In his *Theory of Moral Sentiments* (1812), Smith stated, *"And hence it is, that to feel much for others and little for ourselves, that to restrain our selfish, and to indulge our benevolent affections, constitutes the perfection of human nature; and can alone produce among mankind that harmony of sentiments and passions in which consists their whole grace and propriety."*

Those are lofty ideals, which for centuries our human legacy has clearly not followed.

The present-day world's disparity between nations, classes, races, and gender is staggering, never mind the damage poorly made choices have lain upon our planet. From our past great teachers, we have the knowledge and the means to do right, yet to this day, it's not working.

To counter this condition, some writers and activists seeing capitalism's primary purpose as profit-seeking without social conscious (greed), invented terms, such as "quasi-capitalist" or "profit-diversion capitalism" for individuals or corporations behaving morally as the free market's economic founders intended.

For example:

> *While critics of capitalism may have resigned themselves to its endurance, they have not given up trying to eradicate its perceived flaws. In doing so, they have launched a movement that, in seeking to address these flaws, risks changing the essential character of the market economy. This movement does not seek to dismantle the foundations of capitalism, but rather to transform its goals and basic purpose by proposing new, alternative corporate forms that might best be called "quasi-capitalist.* Sources, National Affairs, *The Dangers of Quasi-Capitalism*, by Howard Husock, winter 2014.

Others, such as Michael Moore, with his movie, *Capitalism: A Love Story,* clearly promotes this negative, greed perspective, an effort appearing hypocritical from which he himself capitalized well.

In this article about Michael Moore in the National Post:

> *He seems to confess that, yes, he is a rich guy after all. But not like other rich guys. He's a rich guy who comes from a working class background, who scraped and scrambled for his money, and who cares. When he sold his first documentary, he recounts, he was paid $3 million and immediately shared the good news with a group of factory workers, students and the unemployed in the middle of the downtown of my birthplace, Flint, Michigan. "I made the decision that if I was going to earn a living, it would be done from my own sweat and ideas and creativity. I would produce something tangible, something others could own or be entertained by or learn from. My work would create employment for others, good employment with middle class wages and full health benefits."* Source; Kelly McParland- Michael Moore explains why he's different from other multi-millionaires. (National Post), Post), Nov 15, 2011

Looking at Mr. Moore's personal sacrifices, actions, and rewards, they mirror exactly what the founders of capitalism intended. Mr. Moore's example is a very positive one of how any real capitalist is supposed to behave.

Under a non-capitalistic economic system, Mr. Moore's earnings would have been deeply cut and redistributed with little remaining of his financial reward, severely reducing his ability to share any good news or to offer help to those in need. Most of the money taken would have supported bureaucrats, offices with only pennies-on-the-dollar remaining to help the needy.

With so many abandoning their moral, free-market obligations, countless similar, incomplete, puerile anti-capitalism examples have arisen.

Thankfully, there is an opportunity for the emergence of a second invisible hand ready to join the free markets' morally-disengaged invisible hand. Currently, it's in a germinal state, and when awakened, these two invisible hands can lift humanity from its slumber into a higher state of awareness and morality, toward economic eudaimonia, ending much global suffering.

This little-known, second, invisible economic hand is explored, defined, and modeled to demonstrate how it can transcend social sympathy from a bottom-up mobilization. To better understand how it can work, a simple understanding of social economics is shared; identifying the underlying factors on why some systems work and others do not. New, simple ideas are offered for needed adjustments, organic in nature and self-operating to make positive changes to existing systems, including world markets, industry, government, social media, and our relationships . . . all toward an autonomous, free, happy, and prosperous planetary economy.

The ideas presented are intended to be a unifying agent, in which the left and right, the atheist and religious, and the rich and the poor can find commonality in our humanity; all timely written for a very needy world.

Some Contextual Frameworks to Be Understood:

- Eudaimonia: Defined by Aristotle as the highest human good in living and flourishing, but not for the self;

- Ethics: A system of moral principles concerned with what is good for individuals and society;

- Freedom and cooperation: Basic moral conduct is required and implied;

- Choice: The essence for success or failure in everything, and it is personal and always by any one person;

- Resources: All our planet/universe has to offer, people, imagination, technology, talent, skills;

- Competition: Defined as an event or contest between people(s). Competition is a component in the free market to ensure the best products, services, and the fairest price but is not the same as capitalism;

- Greed: Defined as a selfish and deep desire for things, such as money, power, and other stuff;

It must be remembered that greed is a choice and not a product, system, or ism.

- Consumerism is not capitalism: Consumerism is an illness, found in any ism where goods abound, and in the extreme, represents a loss in priorities that can be very destructive;

- Commodity: A basic good used in commerce that is interchangeable with other goods of the same type. Commodities are most often used as inputs in the production of other goods or services. The quality of a given commodity may differ slightly, but it is essentially uniform across producers;

Source, Investopedia.com, *What is a Commodity?*, By Jason Fernando, Updated January 04, 2022

- The bad people: Most business owners operate their industries ethically, and many of the rich do much to help the less fortunate. Any harsh sediment expressed in this book is toward those who compromise their responsibilities or sit idly by with great wealth and do nothing. To the public sector individuals who work hard and ethically, you are the examples to be emulated.

Table of Contents

Figures

1

Isms

Eudaimonism, capitalism, Marxism, socialism, communism, imperialism, militarism, fascism, totalitarianism, nationalism, nihilism, Calvinism, regionalism, localism, feminism, conservatism, neo-conservatism, animism, liberalism, egalitarianism, secularism, altruism, environmentalism, anarchism, colonialism, pantheism, creationism, henotheism, ietsism, ignosticism, monotheism, monism, dualism, kathenotheism, omnism, pandeism, panentheism, polytheism, transtheism, trinitarianism, evangelicalism, fundamentalism, occultism, mysticism, neopaganism, atheism, feudalism, humanism, secularism, centralism, apocalypticism, barbarism, humanism, inerrantism, Pentecostalism, premillennialism, revivalism, Unitarianism, catastrophism, consumerism, agnosticism, rationalism, Hinduism, Buddhism, Taoism, Jainism, Judaism, Zionismtheocentrism, Confucianism, Zoroastrianism, Sikhism, Episcopalianism, Catholicism, sacramentalism, Protestantism, Rastafarianism, Presbyterianism, Sufism, Shi'ism, Lutheranism, Unitarianism, Methodism, Puritanism, Mormonism, Seventh-Day Adventism and shamanism, to name just a few.

An ism can be defined as:

> *"taking side with" or "imitation of", and is often used to describe philosophies, theories, religions, social movements, artistic movements and behaviors.*

Source; Oxford English Dictionary online. Oxford: Oxford University Press. 2014

Isms are all around us . . . some purely for dialogue and thought; others are deeply engrained as ideals into the roots of our politics, problem solving, and economics. Others still are blended hybrids, all inadvertently affecting how we interpret and value everything around us. Isms are religious, philosophical, social, political, systemic, and economic.

2

Economic Isms . . . a Simplified Classification

"Let's face it, ideologies are confusing things. The -ism bit seems to make them so very forgettable." Source; *Quick Definitions of Political Ideologies: the –isms*, by Julian Knight

Looking at the different isms of economics from a historical perspective, they seem to have been open-ended experiments, some more gripping than any fiction. Simply put, they can be divided into the ugly, the bad, and hope for the good.

This shift from ugly through bad to good has to do with the type of ism constructed or chosen, where the rules or lack thereof deeply affect the population and planetary interaction. It's interesting how their time-cycle lengths are directly proportionate to the degree from bad to good.

On the chart below, the ugly and good are on opposite poles with bad somewhere in between. It indicates that in a good economy, we are allowed to be free to choose and access our opportunities either available or created. The more controlling, the uglier it becomes, and the harder it is to sustain, resulting in a shorter time frame of operation.

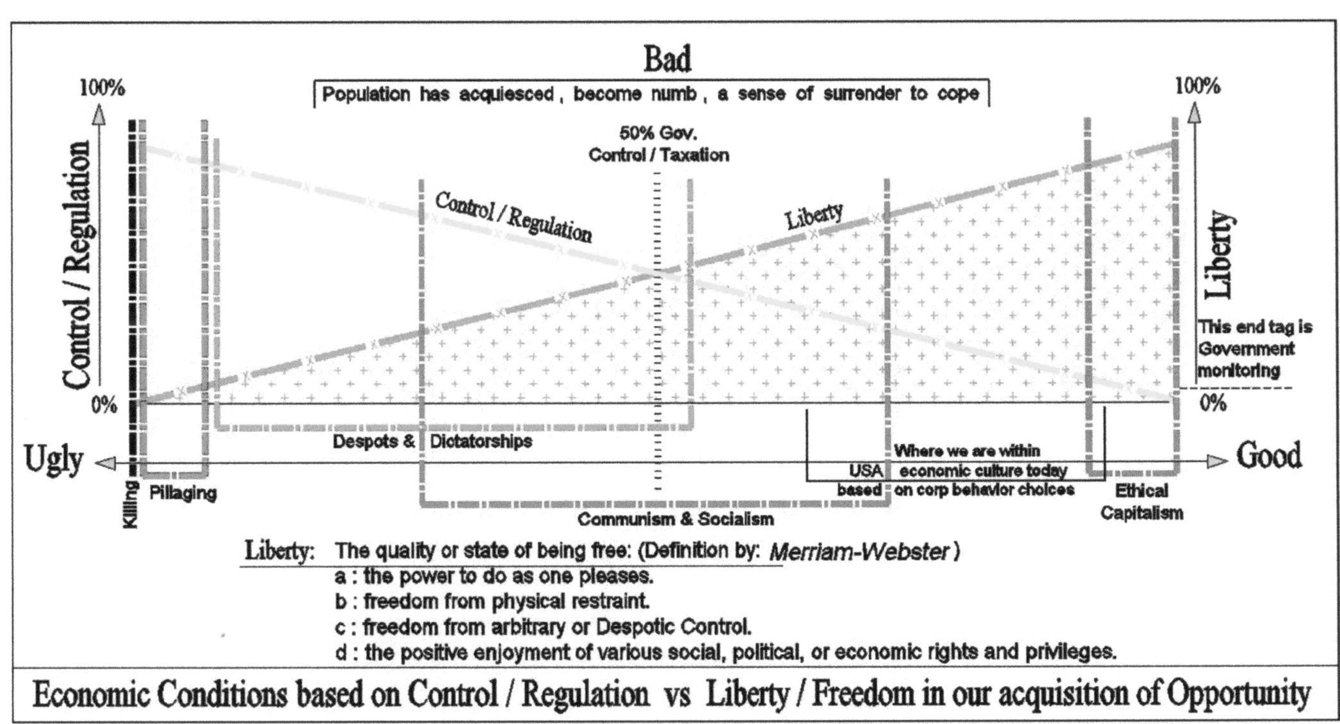

Control/Regulation vs. Liberty/Freedom

2a). The Ugly:

> *"Unpleasant or repulsive, especially in appearance. Involving or likely to involve violence or other unpleasantness."* Source; Oxford Languages

The extreme ugly side of the chart includes societies founded on theft and murder, expending the least economic effort to obtain the resources; that is, actions taken in a very short time frame, commonly associated with foreign invasions, pillaging, clear-cut deforestation, unchecked toxic dumping, and many other dark methods.

In these situations, those taking charge have unfettered control and quickly seize opportunities to strip or destroy the receptor by taking their resources and freedoms, be it people or our environment.

The history of Ireland is a prime example of this oppression. From the 700s to 1760 CE, the island and people were conquered by endless invasions. These started with waves of raids by the Vikings, who, for two centuries, ferociously looted, pillaged, and plundered Ireland. After the Vikings, further attacks were made by the Normans, Scottish, Tudors, Spanish, and English as described here:

> *"English parliamentarian Oliver Cromwell invaded Ireland in 1649 with his New Model Army, hoping to seize Ireland from the ruling Irish Catholic Confederation. By 1652 most of the country had been taken, but pockets of guerrilla rebels endured. Cromwell employed unprecedentedly brutal tactics to defeat them. Estimates of the drop in the Irish population resulting from Cromwell's genocidal campaign sometimes range as high as 50%. The Parliamentarians also deported about 50,000 people as indentured laborers to the Caribbean."* Source: *A coveted island: Nine times Ireland has been invaded, conquered and occupied*, by: Irish Post, October 19, 2016

2b). The Bad:

> *"Of poor quality or a low standard. Not such as to be hoped for or desired; unpleasant or unwelcome."* Source; Oxford Languages

> *"Such immense power allows for the exploitation of the ruled in a way that inflicts violence, both physical and psychological, on its victims. In so doing, it denies individuals opportunities for human development and agency, and thus ultimately robs them of their human dignity. It terrifies all who might oppose it as it is often murderously oppressive."* Source; *Despotism Is All Around Us,* By Vickie B. Sullivan, January 23, 2018

Bad economies, as described above, allow limited individual freedom by controlling though fear and regulation. These run a little longer, usually one lifetime, or increased by the despot's chief side-kicks or offspring becoming the successor. A sure sign of these bad economies is the resultant murder, poverty, disease, and starvation amongst the population caused by those in control. Various degrees of these conditions can be found anywhere on the Control vs. Liberty chart except in the extreme two sides. Life goes on but always under fear with limited empathy from the ruling party or individual.

Sadly, in the present day, many tyrannical nations still exist. According to Planet Rulers, *Current Heads of State & Dictators* of 2020, *"As of today, there are 50 dictatorships in the world (19 in Sub-Saharan Africa, 12 in the Middle East and North Africa, 8 in Asia-Pacific, 7 in Eurasia, 3 in Americas and 1 in Europe). We define a dictator as the ruler of a land rated "Not Free" by the Freedom House in their annual survey of freedom."*

Small tyrannical type rule can also be found in violent gang-run inner cities around the world, often sprung from ghetto life, yielding unbridled crime and murder.

One of the worst historic examples of dictatorial rule was in China, under the despotic leadership of Mao Zedong, from 1949 to 1976, according to *The World's Most Notorious Despots,* by Borgna Brunner of Infoplease, extracted, February 28, 2017:

> *Mao subjected the Chinese people to his massive social experiments, all of which went catastrophically amok. Early in his reign, he encouraged free speech in an attempt to avoid the mistakes of Stalinism. When criticism of his regime arose, however, his true sentiments? Absolute intolerance of dissent and opposition emerged, and he retaliated savagely. When he launched the Great Leap Forward, his economic plan to forge an industrial revolution in China, it resulted in the worst famine of the century, described as a "totally unnecessary, entirely man-made holocaust that claimed between 23 million and 30 million lives." He then masterminded the Cultural Revolution, which, despite its ideological claim to "purify" communism of bureaucrats and elitists, was a vehicle for settling Mao's personal scores and shoring up power. During the nightmarish decade when culture was equated with depravity, millions? Most of whom were guilty of the crime of belonging to the bourgeoisie? Were imprisoned, tortured, and murdered as suspected class enemies.*

Another example was in Ukraine in 1932, under Joseph Stalin's Russian rule. According to the *Holodomor genocide question,* found in Wikipedia:

> *In 1932–33, famine killed 3.3-3.9 million people in Ukraine, included in a total of 5.5-6.5 million killed by the broader Soviet*

> *famine. At least 3.3 million ethnic Ukrainians were among the victims. Scholars continue to debate "whether the man-made Soviet famine was a central act in a campaign of genocide, or whether it was designed to simply cow Ukrainian peasants into submission, drive them into the collectives and ensure a steady supply of grain for Soviet industrialization.*

Under Joseph Stalin's totalitarian rule from 1930 to 1953, of the 18 million people who passed through his gulag system, over 1.5 million people died from the terrible incarceration conditions.

A silent type of the "bad" all around us today can be found in all economies with the super-rich, who have millions of times more money than any one person needs. They may not directly cause the symptoms of poverty, disease, and starvation amongst the population, but they sit by, idly knowingly and watching it all play out when so much suffering could be eased with relatively little charity from these individuals. It's a silent immorality by ignoring one's responsibility to help, perhaps by making up internal stories to explain and justify their non-participation. These individuals are similar to the despots who gather their wealth from the peoples for themselves while the surrounding population suffers.

Bad economic structures grow from the mentality of one or a few individuals who use human life and planetary resources to satisfy their immediate elitism, the antithesis of service, sharing, cooperation, freedom, liberty, and morality.

2c). The Good and the Need for Eudaimonia:

Good is defined as "*That which is morally right; righteousness. Benefit or advantage to someone or something.*" Source; Oxford Languages

Eudaimonia, also spelled eudaemonia, in Aristotelian ethics, the condition of human flourishing or of living well. The conventional English translation of the ancient Greek term, "happiness," is unfortunate because eudaimonia, as Aristotle and most other ancient philosophers understood it, does not consist of a state of mind or a feeling of pleasure or contentment, as "happiness" (as it is commonly used) implies. For Aristotle, eudaimonia is the highest human good, the only human good that is desirable for its own sake (as an end in itself) rather than for the sake of something else (as a means toward some other end). According to Aristotle, every living or human-made thing, including its parts, has a unique or characteristic function or activity that distinguishes it from all other things. The highest good of a thing consists of the good performance of its characteristic function, and the virtue or excellence of a thing consists of whatever traits or qualities enable it to perform that function well. (Thus, the virtue or excellence of a knife is whatever enables the good performance of cutting, that of an eye whatever enables the good performance of seeing, and so on.) It follows that eudaimonia consists of the good performance of the characteristic function of human beings, whatever that may be, and human virtue or excellence is that combination of traits or qualities that enables humans to perform that function well. Aristotle believes that the characteristic function of human beings, that which distinguishes them from all other things, is their ability to reason. Accordingly, "if the function of man is an activity of soul which follows or implies a rational principle," and if the human good is the good performance of that function, then the "human good turns out to be [rational] activity of soul in accordance with virtue," or rational activity performed virtuously or excellently" Source: (*Nichomachean Ethics*, Book I, chapter 7). By Duignan, Brian. Eudaimonia". Encyclopedia Britannica, 3 Jul. 2020, https://www.britannica.com/topic/eudaimonia.

Based on logic, virtue, and purpose, the eudaimonia condition is essential to any good economy . . . within a safe and ethical economic culture, individuals are free to explore and develop themselves and their passions, be it in the arts, sciences, or industry. So not to burden the people with heavy taxation and be inherently transparent, this system would require a small government. A government that, on one hand, ensures the people and planet are protected, and on the other, is swift to carry out justice should social trusts be broken. These structures will be further explored and modeled later.

With our horrific social/economic history of dictatorships, corruption, and the current economic disparity, these aspirations appear utopian. But with some simple checks and balances, the free market's *invisible hand,* along with leaders of the government and industry, can be steered toward a stable and moral path. These checks and balances must come from the bottom up to preserve freedom and encourage cooperation, thereby maximizing morally grounded choices toward everyone's opportunity for a fulfilling and meaningful life.

Today, there are no "good" economies as described above. For a glimpse of our current condition, see the global map in the Greed and Corruption section. Sadly, even countries with minimally strong economies have the 'billionaire-poverty' disparity, yielding grounds for social-economic instability almost everywhere.

3

Sustainability and Economics

This new world should be the world in which the strong won't exploit the weak, the bad won't exploit the good, where the poor won't be humiliated by the rich. It will be the world in which the children of intellect, science and skills will serve to the community in order to make lives easier and nicer. And not to the individuals for gaining wealth. This new world can't be the world of the humiliated, the broken but the world of free people and nations equal in dignity and respect for man. —Nikola Tesla

The different approaches to economic means all vary in degrees of control versus freedom and, as mentioned, the uglier economy always has less freedom and less stability. To hold these social/economic structures together, they require more rules, regulation, and imposed fear and money, resulting in less resources and freedom for the people, eventually leading to social unrest and making the cycle proportionality shorter. These types of economies can run for many generations, but, in reality, are artificially sustained from the suffering of its citizens . . . sadly, "fake."

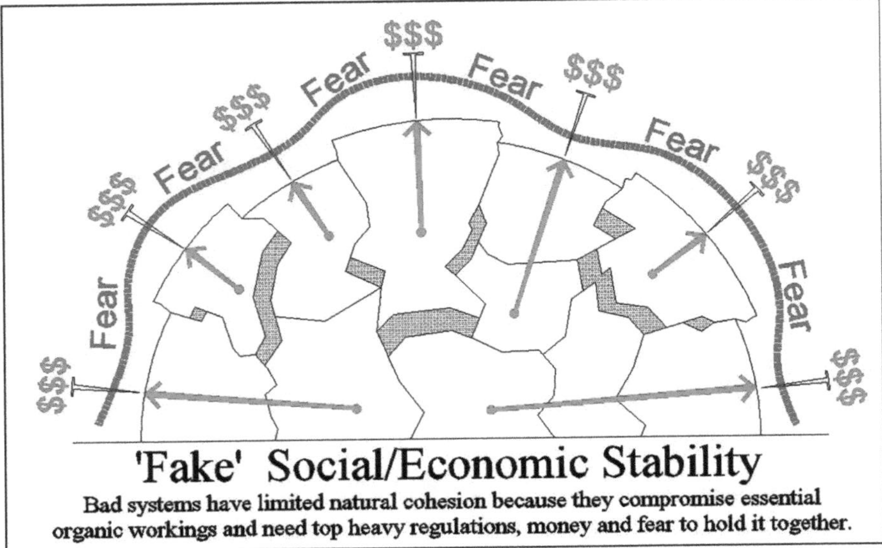
$$$
Fear
$$$
Fear
$$$
Fear
$$$
Fear
$$$
Fear
$$$
Fear
$$$
Fear
$$$
'Fake' Social/Economic Stability
Bad systems have limited natural cohesion because they compromise essential organic workings and need top heavy regulations, money and fear to hold it together.

In the diagram below, systems with more cooperative freedom can relieve many social stresses, thereby yielding longer time frames, making them more sustainable. Heavily controlled economic methods that restrict the people have higher stresses and end up in shorter time frames of operation. The uglier the means of economic methods always have higher stresses on their resources, making them less sustainable, and the cycle concludes quicker. Oppressed people and a scorched earth are never happy outcomes.

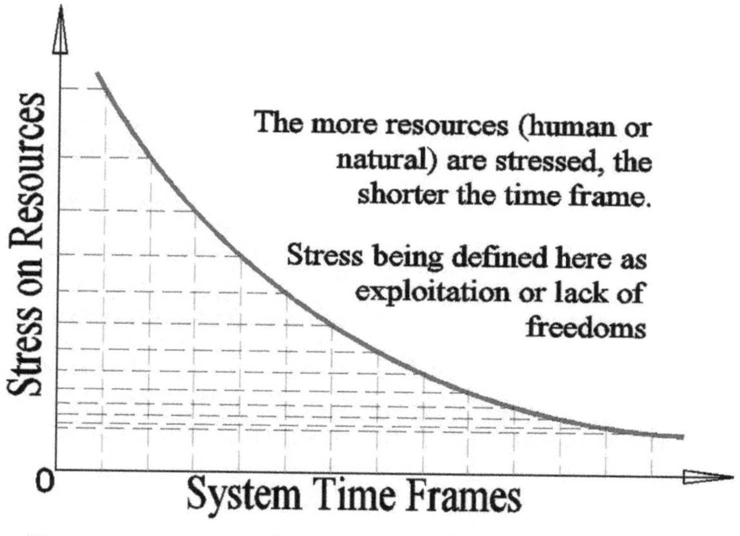
Stress on Resources
The more resources (human or natural) are stressed, the shorter the time frame.
Stress being defined here as exploitation or lack of freedoms
0
System Time Frames
Resource Abuse vs Sustainability

Happier economic systems allow the populations to make their own choices for opportunity and the means to realize them within a culture of cooperation. When freedom abounds, isms always last longer . . . to do so, they must have an inner organic structure that allows them to basically run themselves and so requiring less cost for sustainability. It must be understood that extreme liberty void of virtue and principle is chaos, devoid of morality, making a state of freedom untenable.

4

Free Market

It [the free market] is an organizational way of doing things, featuring openness, which enables millions of people to cooperate and compete without demanding a preliminary clearance of pedigree, nationality, color, race, religion, or wealth. It demands only that each person abide by voluntary principles, that is, by fair play. The free market means willing exchange; it is impersonal justice in the economic sphere and excludes coercion, plunder, theft, protectionism, and other anti-free market ways by which goods and services change hands. Quote by Leonard Read (1898-1983) author and founder of the Foundation for Economic Education.

"The free market punishes irresponsibility. Government rewards it." Quote by Harry Browne (1933-2006), American writer, politician, and investment analyst.

The foundations for capitalism provided by its founders recognized the importance of the invisible hand as an essential part for the free market to work.

For those with little economic knowledge, here's a quick Economics 101.

The invisible hand, as described by Adam Smith (1723–90), referred to here is a metaphor of how the free market works. For example, say you start a business-making widget-A, but you're not the only one making these, your price and quality has to be as good or better than the other business; otherwise, the invisible hand will remove your ability to earn a living. Then, you invent a better widget-A, and for less money. Now, by the invisible hand, your business grows. Another twist could come with new technology. Old technologies or widgets would be abandoned, and the new would prosper with this invisible hand ensuring a fair price and quality product, determining equilibrium in the supply and demand for goods. All this happens on its own, free of government regulation, founded within an inseparable context of ethics and morality.

Observing our past and current times, we see the essential moral component for many has run unchecked, be it capitalism, socialism, or communism, all leading to a small number of people within their isms, amassing huge fortunes while so many around the world suffer in extreme poverty, misery, and disease.

The current leanings toward socialism, where the government regulates economic fairness, requires top-heavy structure, reducing the working people's freedoms through regulation and higher taxation to feed the resultant larger government, leaving only a small percentage of those tax dollars taken to actually help the less fortunate. (See Our Tax Dollar.) Also, adding government regulation will stifle the self-acting, invisible hand.

It's clear that greed and the hunger for power are the problem, issues which no government structures can change. The history of socialism, a system that is supposed to have minimal economic disparity, always has rich leaders. The leaders make these rules for the "good of the people" but don't follow them themselves.

Here are some examples:

In socialist Venezuela: *"The majority of Venezuelans are struggling to survive as the country has become engulfed in 'poverty and political violence' but this only applies for some. The wealthy minority still sip cocktails, enjoy nights at the bar and eat sushi as they live unfazed by the turmoil outside their walls."* Source: Forbes, *Venezuela's Rich Aren't Suffering–That's Why Socialism's Such A Bad Idea, The Poor Do,* by Tim Worstall, Jun 21, 2017

Fidel Castro, "Cuba's long-time leader, who was prime minister of the Caribbean country from 1959 to 1976 and president from 1976 to 2008, may have espoused Marxist-Leninist values based on fair distribution of wealth, but that didn't stop him apparently accruing an immense personal fortune. In 2006, his net worth was estimated by Forbes at $900 million. When adjusted for inflation, that's $1.15 billion." Source: https://www.lovemoney.com/, *The richest world leaders of all time. Extracted June 05, 2021*

"China's premier from 2003 to 2013, Wen Jiabao managed to stockpile billions during his 10-year term. A comprehensive review of company and regulatory filings published in the New York Times in 2012 revealed the Communist Party of China chief had garnered assets amounting to $2.7 billion." Source: https://www.lovemoney.com/, *The richest world leaders of all time. Extracted June 05, 2021*

It's reported that the African Gabonese Socialist Union leader, "*Gabonese president Ali Bongo Ondimba may have siphoned off 25% of his country's gross domestic product, so it's highly likely the politician, who has been in power since 2009, is worth significantly more than the $2 billion figure that is widely quoted. His assets include a $138 million townhouse in Paris."* Source: https://www.lovemoney.com/, *The richest world leaders of all time. Extracted June 05, 2021*

In the US, some of the present-day politicians and lawmakers who support socialist views are rich and got so under a free-market economy. Some want all of us to equalize our wealth, but will they throw themselves into that same pool?

After extensive research, all socialist persons of high power were found to be rich. It would take a real saint of a leader to give up their wealth like the citizens are required to do by law when they have the power to acquire and also get away with keeping it.

So where do we turn? In a quote from Winston Churchill, *"It has been said that democracy is the worst form of government except all the others that have been tried."* Source: https://richardlangworth.com , Worst Form of Government.

5

Interactions and Free Choice

To find any solution, one must first ask the right question. This question about free choice goes back to the garden of Eden, a very old one . . . how do you control free choice and still keep it free?

This is an obvious contradiction, rendering it seemingly unworkable. Many isms of the past tried to capture this missing link with different degrees of freedom, interaction, and regulation. Some tried through heavy-handed government control, and others with little to none. Neither extreme has ever worked, but was there something missing, and is there a possible equilibrium for future functionality?

Regulation stifles freedom, and absence of rules can lead to anarchy. So how can a society have order and feel free to choose to live to the full extent of their dreams and efforts on a safe and healthy planet?

Let's break social/economic systems down to most basic bare essentials to find the weak link for success or failure. Be it government, business, or personal. Every social/economic system has two-root human components:

1. The need to interact
2. The need for a choice

Interaction between each other and the planet is the root of economics, and we have no choice but to do so. For example, if we decide to self-isolate, we still need to eat, breathe, and reproduce for that economy to continue, all of which are interactions. So the only human economic variable that we have control over is our free choice. This means the historic and present day's economic successes or failings have only to do with someone's excellent or poor choices. One could argue that some past economic failings resulted from environmental disasters or shortages; but these were usually short-lived and often caused by man-made poor choices. So the solution must lie within this variable of choice.

With our choices being the only thing we have control over, what would the best choice be? The best choices would most likely be those that lead to more choices. The more choices, the more robust our diversity for opportunity is in everything, including our economy. Choices that enhance our resources, including our workplaces and our planet, making humanity broader and stronger, are always the best. See the "Full Spectrum of Interaction" diagram on page 21. To ensure the best product or service within a legal/ethical set of rules to protect against fraud, theft, price hiking, and so on, these choices, as demonstrated on the previous charts, can only involve a competitive free market.

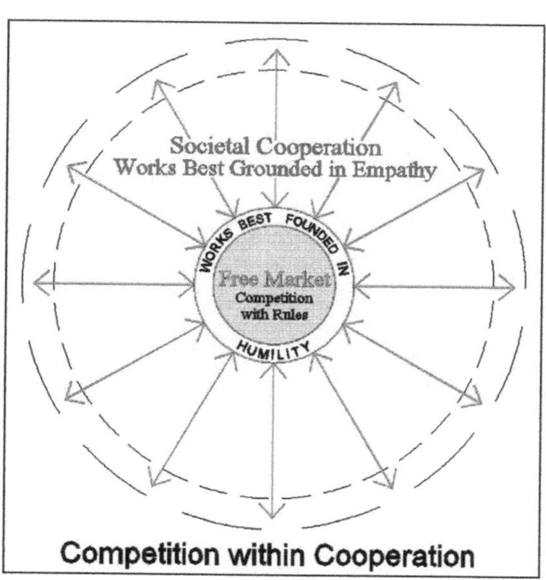

Competition within Cooperation

Notice the free market in the diagram above is incased in a circle of humility. The need for this growing awareness yields the best performance personally, in business, and our cultures, just as cooperation is best grounded in empathy.

Humility is the conductor required for all other virtues to be expressed in the human world, limited only by the capacity discovered within each of us through daily life choices.

> *"Larger-than-life egos are fast becoming liabilities. Indeed, in what may first appear to be a paradox, ego's mortal enemy—humility—is one of the traits most likely to guarantee success in the 21st century workplace."* Source; In Business Greater Phoenix, by Edward D. Hess, *Humility Is the New Key to Success,* January 2016

> *"Competition tends to create greater cooperation, and greater cooperation makes you more competitive. Social species are so common because cooperation makes it more likely your genes will be passed on. In evolution, it is really survival of the most cooperative."* Source; By Troy Camplin, *Competition vs. Cooperation,* Jan 14, 2020

Sorry, but Darwin got it wrong. In the big picture, we are stronger together rather than at each other's throats.

The chart below shows how interaction can morph into two directions based on our choices. These can be spontaneous choices or those in written policy by business or government, but they are always made by an individual . . . a personal choice.

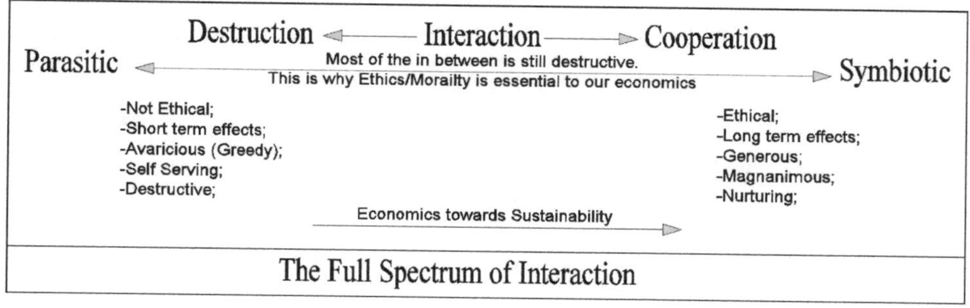

The Full Spectrum of Interaction

The above diagram indicates most of the middle is destructive, indicating that we have to stay very much to its symbiotic side. Actions as simple as one bad lie, the mishandling of toxic waste, or one bad policy, just to list a few, can have dismal consequences.

We can choose selfishness, evil, benevolence, charity, encouragement, commodity, wisdom, or kindness. The virtue or lack thereof we pick is up to any of us and forms any economy's outcome from the micro to the macro.

Our created societal structures (again, from choices made by someone) can force the appearance of cooperation through fear and bad law as demonstrated in the "fake" social/economic diagram, while real cooperation springs from free choice, is naturally nurturing and usually enjoyable. The cooperation expressed here is for the good of society and not for deception. Real cooperation cannot be regulated; it is spirited and comes from the heart. Regulated cooperation is impossible, as it would then be a form of enforcement, undermining the sense of freedom.

Extreme regulations are analogous to shotgun marriages. Better societal structures allow for the organic growth of a free hand for choice and action. Free choice always springs from a desire and hope for opportunity. Understand, "free choice" intended here is that which does not harm us, others, or our planet.

In a perfect world, the best possible economic structure would maximize cooperation within an ethical free market, encouraging individual moral choices to ever expand individual opportunities in the exploration, acquisition, and development of their choices for the best sustainable use of any resource toward the betterment of society and the planet.

In regards to civilization, Mahatma Gandhi said, *"To observe morality is to attain mastery over our mind and our passions. So doing, we know ourselves."* Source, Collected Works of Mahatma Gandhi: Vol. 10: 279, (Aug 5, 1909–Apr 9, 1910)

For any group of people to be considered civilized, their community must address these challenges. The definition of civilization, found in the yourdictionary.com is: *"Showing evidence of moral and intellectual advancement; humane, reasonable, ethical."* Source: The American Heritage Dictionary of the English Language, fifth edition. Copyright © 2016, 2011 by Houghton Mifflin Harcourt Publishing Company.

The ethical failings throughout history and our current societies leave the door open for much-needed improvements.

6

Societal Change

"What causes societal change? Four common causes, as recognized by social scientists, are technology, social institutions, population, and the environment. All four of these areas can impact when and how society changes." Source; Britannica.com

Our world today is clearly in need of change but not so much from externalities but rather from within itself through a cultural shift with a larger awareness from new information/knowledge to reprioritize our current attitudes and values for what works best with our planet, society, and economics.

There are three elements required for the founding and operation of any societal system:

1. The ideal:
According to Merriam-Webster, an ideal is defined as *"a standard of perfection, beauty, or excellence: one regarded as exemplifying an ideal and often taken as a model for imitation: an ultimate object or aim of endeavor: goal."* Source: www.merriam-webster.com/dictionary/ideal.

2. Virtue:
According to Merriam-Webster, a virtue is defined as *"the quality of being morally good. . . . The word virtue comes from the Latin root vir, for man. At first virtue meant manliness or valor, but over time it settled into*

the sense of moral excellence." Source: www.merriam-webster.com/dictionary/virtue.

3. Principles:
A principle can be defined as *"A fundamental truth or proposition that serves as the foundation for a system of belief or behavior or for a chain of reasoning."* Source: www.lexico.com/definition/principle.

In a societal-structure metaphor, the ideal can be seen as the dream, the virtue as the tool/mechanism and principle as the human value or choice. All isms are built on these three, and the test of time always shows a societal ism's success or failure.

6a). The Ideal:

> *"Our heritage and ideals, our code and standards – the things we live by and teach our children – are preserved or diminished by how freely we exchange ideas and feelings."* —Walt Disney

Choose a poor ideal, and the ism fails right off. No one is excited, and it ends there. Good ideals take on a momentum of their own; like an invisible power, they are quickly accepted and disseminated. Good ideals, by their nature, allow virtues to align and compliment. Other ideals can appear good on the surface and can continue operating for decades, but if their inner nature undermines basic virtues, they will eventually implode, always at much cost and suffering. See the "Fake Social/Economic Stability" diagram on page 12.

An example of this type of ideal failure was witnessed with Karl Marx and communism. Ideals of equality for all, a lofty sounding ideal that was wheeled with power and authority, pushed from the top-down on all. According to this article in USA Today, *Don't celebrate Karl Marx. His Communism has a death count in the millions.* by James

Bovard, May 05, 2018. *"Marxism in practice didn't work out so well. Communist regimes produced the greatest ideological carnage in human history, killing more than a hundred million people in the last century."*

Marxism as an ideal embraced several virtues, including trust and fairness, intended to increase the principles and values of compassion, sharing, caring, helping the poor, and yet failed miserably, resulting in the unfathomable death and grotesque wealth for the government officials administrating it.

A similar history can be seen with religious movements. Originating over millennia with their failings, beginning when these movements originally founded on a pure, messianic ideal, made their ideal into an idol, forgoing the associated virtues, falling into the depths of building power structures, kept alive through fear, control, corruption and murder, all hypocritical in the name of God.

6b). Virtues:

> *"Respect for self is the beginning of cultivating virtue in men and women."* Gordon B. Hinckley, an American religious leader

> *"The order of nature is that individual happiness shall be inseparable from the practice of virtue."* Quote by Thomas Jefferson

Today, virtuous systems have three sources:

1. Supernatural virtues: From prophets who emphasized, most under severe oppression, that their knowledge and words were not their own but came from a spiritual realm or God. Witnesses claim these prophets all exhibited superhuman knowledge and abilities, many called miracles. These virtues are from the religious arm, and

the sources of many pre-date any historic records and are deeply ingrained into all cultures.

2. Classical virtues: Explored and documented by philosophers, sages, and elders. Many of the virtues are similar to the supernatural; for example, according to Aristotle: courage, temperance, ambitiousness, friendliness, and gentleness, generosity, magnificence, magnanimity, truthfulness, wittiness, justice/fairness, knowledge, intellect, and wisdom.

3. Secular virtue: These are more recent, based on academic study and not upon holy or classical texts.

For example, in the book, *How Good People Make Tough Choices: Resolving the Dilemmas of Ethical Living*, Rushworth Kidder identifies four general characteristics of an ethical code:

1. *It is brief;*
2. *It is usually not explanatory;*
3. *Can be expressed in a number of forms (e.g. positive or negative, single words or a list of sentences); and*
4. *Centers on moral values.* SOURCE; Kidder 2003. 82, Jan, 2006.

Whatever the source, it cannot be denied that the existence of virtues percolates all cultures, religious or not, and all are intended toward a better end. Virtues are humans' societal hard wiring. It protects our communities and cultures from chaos/anarchy and allows them to prosper.

As previously mentioned, for success, the ideal and its inherent virtues of any ism must complement for them to work and always involve a combination of virtues. For example, knowledge without temperance can lead to arrogance, or generosity without wisdom can lead to destitution. It's similar to a cooking recipe. Miss one ingredient, and the soufflé will not rise. Isms that naturally allow its ideal to stand upon virtues will do better than those that don't as history is a testament. The ideal-ideal would, by its very nature, nurture a state of free cooperation, requiring minimal third party imposition. In other words, the good ideal's essence internally nurtures itself to ethically grow as it is intended to do, leading to higher stability, efficiencies, and better economics.

6c). Principles:

> *"The solutions to our problems are and always will be based upon universal, timeless, self-evident principles common to every enduring, prospering society throughout history."* Quote by Stephen R. Covey, an American educator, author, businessman

Principles are very important in relation to ethics, as they guide us in the use of our tools. For example, a car driven by a reckless driver can result in death; those who use money for evil and corruption is another example; those who use drugs in a way not intended, and the list goes on forever. Tools are not good or evil as they have no conscience; it's how we choose to use the tools; it is always the individual who wield any tool and choose to do good or bad.

A simple example of how virtues are societal tools needing principle is someone with tremendous knowledge-virtue, yet lacking in principle, which is more dangerous than someone with less knowledge-virtue. These types are often portrayed as the super-villains in comic books and movies.

Principles are all about value choices. By making principled choices, we can reflect the intended qualities of virtue, toward an ideal, essential for good civilization and economics as indicated here.

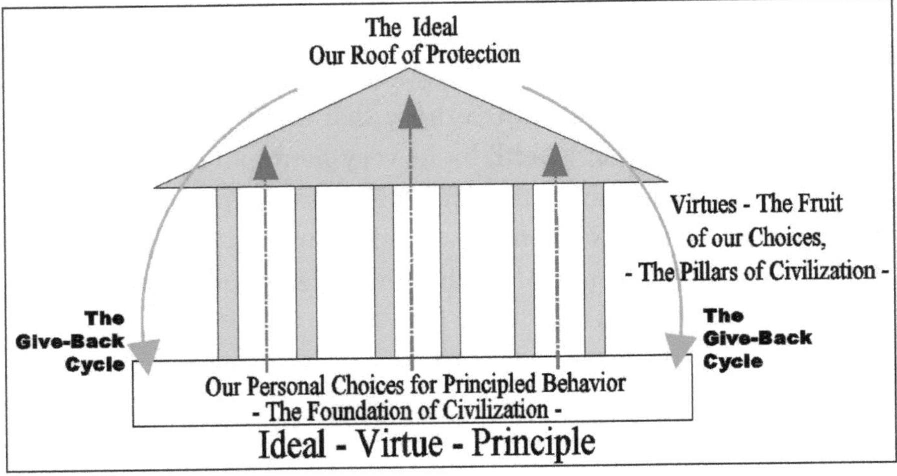

In the above diagram, for good civilization and economics to work, the foundation is our principled choices; virtues are the pillars, and the ideal is our roof (our protection). A healthy working society is dependent on the successful individuals to share their excessive fruits back to the foundation to keep the cycle going. Sharing our excessive fruits is an essential moral obligation, which includes internal capacities/resources and not just money. Isn't this what we were all taught in kindergarten? Imagine our world today if the likes of Newton, Einstein, Tesla, and so on decided not to share their inner gifts? Individuals with excess have a moral responsibility to share. This always works best when done altruistically rather than via external third party forces.

It is always the individual and not a government or corporate committee who makes the choice of how to use a tool. It is always each of us, the individual in that quiet moment inside the deepest part of ourselves, and when we find ourselves in a situation requiring a choice. This would include writing any policy . . . be it good or bad; it's always some individual making that choice.

The Crossroads of Personal Choice

It's an ancient dilemma found throughout all human ages and cultures. Each of us have this power to change or influence toward the better or worse through our personal choices, which, when principled, are directly proportional to the excess capacities/resource we were given or have amassed. Having more is not some gift to smile about; rather, it's a greater responsibility to share.

7

The Religious vs. Secular Divide

"But what if the conviction that religion and secularism are intractable adversaries is mistaken? What if a certain disabling dogmatism afflicts both the religious spirit and the secular spirit? What if reexamination of traditional religious sources and of seminal works of secularism revealed that both contained an openness to, and even imperative to consider respectfully and learn from, the achievements of the other?" Source; *Bridging the Religious-Secular Divide*, a commentary by Peter Berkowitz, extracted August 20, 2021

So what does this have to do with economics? The religious versus the secular, historically and still today, have always played a huge part in economics, making it an essential component to explore. Without solid ethics, much of which came from religion, the foundations of economic structures suffer. Also, from where and how we interpret our world has all to do with our social and economic structuring, much of which is currently in flux.

Today, societies have simply turned a blind eye to so many economic injustices, including greed, environmental harm, work conditions, and so on, leading to the growth of a secular, socialist type movement against the foundations of the supernatural and free-market economic structures, blaming capitalism, corporations, and religions as the problem source. What's being missed in some of these types of movements is an in-depth understanding of our ethics, beneath the obvious superficial equalization rants, very similar to Marxist type ideals. Has the history of this terrible example already been forgotten so that we can repeat the destruction previously witnessed?

Even with these strong secular, socialist type movements, as of 2012, it was estimated that most people of the world still considered themselves religious.

> *Nonreligious include agnostic, atheist, secular, humanist, and people answering 'none' or no religious preference. Half of this group is theistic but nonreligious. According to a 2012 study by Gallup International "59% of the world said that they think of themselves as religious person, 23% think of themselves as not religious whereas 13% think of themselves as convinced atheists."* Source, "*Global Index of Religion and Atheism: Press Release*" (PDF). Archived from the original (PDF) on 16 October 2012.

But it appears the secular movement is rapidly expanding:

> *Data for the USA suggest that the prevalence of atheism has increased rapidly in the 21st century from around 6% to 23% and the prevalence of non-religious people has also increased from less than 2% to 12%. The prevalence of irreligion (atheists and non-religious) has increased by an estimated 30 percentage points over the last two decades, the largest increase of any country included in this analysis. Closely behind is South Korea, followed by Iceland, the Netherlands, Spain, Finland, Norway, the UK and Australia (15 percentage point increase). The overall prevalence of irreligion is higher in these other countries, but the USA is catching up.* Source, Religiosity and atheism in 2020, Posted on September 5, 2020 by colinmathers.com.

Besides this secular movement, new discoveries in science have another direction emerging... call it "super science" for interpreting ourselves. Perhaps this type of exploration can play a part to bridge the supernatural with secular gap. For example, *"A team of theoretical physicists working with Microsoft published a paper describing the universe as a self-learning system of evolutionary laws. An idea that we live inside a computer-like universe that continuously learns."* Source: The Autodidactic Universe, Stephon Alexander, William J. Cunningham, Jaron Lanier, Lee Smolin, Stefan Stanojevic, Michael W. Toomey, and Dave Wecker, April 9 2021

With all these diverse contexts, how can we make sense? A great exercise for this situation is to accept that we actually know nothing. Our senses can be fooled like in the cave allegory by the Greek philosopher Plato (+/-428 to +/-347 BCE) in his work Republic (514a–520a), where three individuals living in a cave, relying only on their sight, believed the cave shadows were real entities. Plato argued that we must use philosophical reasoning to find truths and understanding. That we must question everything we assume to be true and call real.

We need to remind ourselves that we know very little in the context of our reality. Following Plato's logic above, the secular will tell the supernatural to give up believing, that it does not exist, and the supernatural will tell the secular that they have closed their minds to an amazing realm. Sadly, this is a rift between half of the world that believes, and the other that does not.

Many of the God believers see and experience the supernatural as a science not yet discovered. For example, if we could bring a computer, cell phone, or jet aircraft back to the Stone Age, it would certainly appear as from an unknown realm to those living then.

Today, the secular often look at the religious population as beneath them, as being victims of ignorant belief systems. But the religious people have their own proofs of historic scripture or visions and unexplainable experiences. Hopefully, the religious will be patient with the secular, and the secular will be more open-minded to the supernatural side. Just as the endless beauty in scientific discovery, there is endless beauty in meditation and the exploration of our spiritual side, and perhaps the very source of our human ability for scientific exploration.

The secular versus the supernatural views lead to many passionate arguments. The danger arises when one side sees itself superior to the other, leading to acts of censorship and reeducation, often times, very subtle, causing one to ask, "How can knowledge be erased or unlearned, and what good does that do?" It's like asking someone to pretend they can no longer read. This restrictive approach attacks freedoms and truly is a form of oppression, breaking virtues, such as love, temperance, wisdom, and diversity, to name a few, leading to unsustainability. There is no happy ending on this path with many examples in the ugly part of our human history.

> *"When one side benefits more than the other, that's a win-lose situation. To the winner it might look like success for a while, but in the long run, it breeds resentment and distrust."* Quote by Stephen R. Covey.

As previously mentioned, diversity of thought is better than restrictions of thought as it is more robust, making society stronger. Crazy, wacky, cult types may attract a few followers, but they generally censor themselves through their own insanity, and should they express violence, the justice system can deal with them. It's much better to keep the First Amendment for the freedom of speech than have a censorship process, under which these types would simply go underground and work from the shadows.

The secular can argue religion has done much harm, but it must be remembered, those religions behaving so are no different than government despots or bad corporations who have also done so much damage. Whether it's government, corporate or religious, those who behaved badly throughout history did so for greed and the lust for power instead of service. Evil is evil; it's not governments, corporations, or religions. It can't be overstated that it's the ruling individuals who make selfish choices; they are the problem more than what they represent. They gave up the original ideal and compromised it for selfish purposes.

The seculars need to understand that the supernatural experience will never disappear for religious people, nor should it. How can the religious be told that their spiritual visions and experiences of lost loved ones are not true or meaningless? There are many testimonials where people were forced to their knees, through the power of holiness, so pure and too overwhelming for a mortal; an unseen force we don't yet understand. Also witnesses to spiritual experiences, where time as a dimension no longer exists, past, present, and future, are one property. Many artists and scientists throughout history state spiritual messages inspired their work. We humans are so complex in both the secular and the spirit.

Some say believing is seeing. Knowledge can sometimes be a block to a new experience or idea. If you believe you have it all figured out, the new or contradictory are not in your sights, and it passes you by. Water always flows to the valley just as new ideas always flow to the humble.

Carl Sagan said, *"The notion that science and spirituality are somehow mutually exclusive does a great disservice to both."*

Jennifer Beals said, *"I think science and spirituality are one and the same. Quantum physics is now validation all kinds of spiritual teachings."*

Albert Einstein said, *"Each of us has to do his little bit toward transforming this spirit of the times."*

John Hagelin said, *"A great unification is now taking place between science and spirituality. The most advanced discoveries of modern science are rising to reaffirm the timeless wisdom of the great religious and spiritual traditions of every culture."*

In the meantime, the current division helps no one, including our economy. For unity and peace, we need to cooperate, regardless of whether we are God believers or not. As rational people, we can observe and predict what works well, better, or worse. No one has to disbelieve or be converted. It's our diversity of thought that makes us strong, just as having a diverse gene pool is biologically healthier. Our genes are our hardware, and our culture is our software. Diversity is always strength, making us more equipped should life's circumstances surprisingly change.

8

So Are We Evil?

This is a big question and one about our human hardwiring; are we greedy/evil by nature? If so, then there is no hope for us, and what is being suggested here is impossible. To build anything beautiful takes much effort and skill. To destroy takes no skill . . . any ignorant person can destroy. Perhaps that's why our history is so full of failure and corruption . . . hard to build, easy to destroy.

> *"I have a little different definition of evil than most people. When you have the opportunity and the ability to do good and you do nothing, that's evil. Evil doesn't always have to be an overt act, it can be merely the absence of good."* Quote by Yvon Chouinard, an American rock climber and environmentalist.

Yvon makes two interesting points here, the first of which can be aimed directly to most of the super-rich, and the other has to do with nature itself.

For example, let's look at these relationships:

1. When there is darkness + light, it always equals light, not grey or some dimness in between.
2. When there is ignorance + knowledge, it is always knowledge, not a portion thereof.
3. When there is cold + heat, the heat energy is not diminished and fully present in that medium.

So when there is evil + virtue, is the goodness transferred and still also fully present in that person? It seems the knowledge type virtues can be transferred, but the moral ones may take more effort, involving principled choices.

> *"Those who are virtuous will find it fairly natural to act morally. . . . While intellectual virtues are learned from teaching, the moral virtues must be developed primarily through practice. Though we all have the potential to develop both vices and virtues, neither virtue nor vice is innate."* Source; Southwest State University, by Hugh Mercer Curtler, *Can Virtue Be Taught?* Volume VII, No. 1, 1994

The dark side of this "evil" argument is the belief that we have a "selfish gene," made popular by British atheist writer Richard Dawkins, in his book *The Selfish Gene*, Oxford University Press, 1976, suggesting we only behave kindly for selfish, ulterior motives and that our evolutionary rising came out of intense competition for food and water, to accumulate power and possessions, ingraining ruthlessness into our very being—the opposite of eudaimonism.

However, Steve Taylor PhD, in an article called *An Alternative View of Human Nature*, found on www.psychologytoday.com, posted July 20, 2018, points out that in our prehistoric times, our population was very small and the resources vast, and so why would we have to be ruthless in such a world? As Dr. Taylor points out, if we did, it would be simply for the sport as private property, or ownership did not exist. He explains how a competitive state of being would not be very conducive to a fledgling species trying to survive. He also points out how present-day hunter and gathering communities all demonstrate strong egalitarianism between themselves and the sharing of their resources. They are more cooperative than competitive, even ridiculing those who become too boastful.

Historically, the best economies came about from the tide of good deeds rather than chasing profits. The historic golden ages all blossomed from a population uplifted through some ideal to give back, provide service to their communities, and advance the arts and sciences, through which the general public and leadership strived for betterment, causing their economies and cultures to flourish. Again, cooperation, service, striving, and sacrifice from the grassroots, from one's sense of freedom and liberty and not by forced legislature.

Our trust with each other, with justification through our good nature as a cooperating species, is the best explanation of how our species came through past natural and manmade catastrophes. They would have formed moral/ethical boundaries, which became deeply embedded in our human cultures. We all have a hunger for dignity. It's one of the most gratifying feelings of reward, and in books or movies, we immediately know the good from the bad, with most of us identifying with the good person and their deeds rather than the evil one.

> *So there is no reason to think that selfishness and cruelty are natural to human beings. There is no reason why traits such as racism, warfare, and male domination should have been selected by evolution since they would have had no benefit to us. In fact, as we have seen, individuals who behaved selfishly and ruthlessly would be less likely to survive, since they would have been ostracized from their groups. On the contrary, it makes more sense to see traits such as cooperation, egalitarianism, altruism, and peacefulness as natural to human beings. These were the traits that have been prevalent in human life for tens of thousands of years. So presumably these traits are still strong in us now.* Source, Steve Taylor Ph.D. Kindness and cooperation are more natural to human beings than selfishness. Posted July 20, 2018.

These are some images reflecting the better nature of humankind:

This chalk sign was found at an entrance to a restaurant.

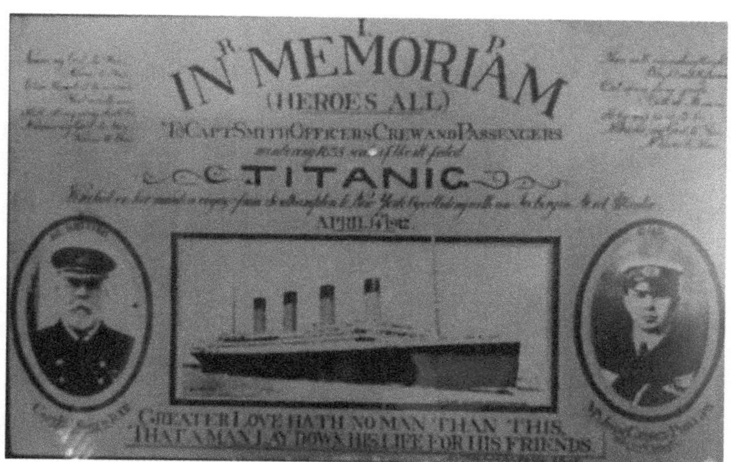

Titanic in Memoriam

> *"Greater love hath no man than this that a man laydown his life for his friends."* Source, King James Bible John 15:13

Historically, there have been some noble leaders who, through their personal sacrifices, choices of good character, and wisdom, built and left legacies of advancement, innovation, and arts for their civilizations. For example, *"Charlemagne (742-814), or Charles the Great, was king of the Franks, 768-814, and emperor of the West, 800-814. He founded the Holy Roman Empire, stimulated European economic and political life, and fostered the cultural revival known as the Carolingian Renaissance."*

Source: Encyclopedia.com, extracted June 6, 2021

> *"According to John Contreni, 'it had a spectacular effect on education and culture in Francia, a debatable effect on artistic endeavors, and an immeasurable effect on what mattered most to the Carolingians, the moral regeneration of society'"* Source: Wikipedia, extracted June 6, 2021.

Another example was under the rule of the Abbasid caliphs in 762 CE; they brought in the Golden Age of Islam and established the city of Baghdad, a center of learning, science, and arts. They also put together a group of scholars they called the House of Wisdom to oversee many great projects and endeavors.

> *"A love of knowledge was evident in Baghdad, established in 762 CE as the capital city of the Abbasid Caliphate in modern-day Iraq. Scholars, philosophers, doctors, and other thinkers all gathered in this center of trade and cultural development. Academics—many of them fluent in Greek and Arabic—exchanged ideas and translated Greek texts into Arabic."* Source: https://www.khanacademy.org, extracted June 8, 2021

Voluntary sharing, historically, has always been an important part of any healthy civilization. It only takes one virtuous hero with power or wealth to make a huge difference to their community or nation. These charismatic leaders raised ideals of hope and prospect, inspiring the peoples to take up the torch and share their efforts and skills to make a difference for society's improvements in arts and sciences, their work being reminders to the living to join in, share our excesses, or sacrifice for good influence during our short existence.

Wikipedia defines society as, *"a group of individuals involved in persistent social interaction, or a large social group sharing the same spatial or social territory, typically subject to the same political authority and dominant cultural expectations."* Source: https://artsandculture.google.com/entity/society/m098wr?hl=en.

Today, those with the means need to participate in their capacities for the sake of much-needed global improvement. There are always many small to middle power players and a couple big ones doing their part, but today, where are the silent super-rich, and will they ever morally volunteer their wisdom or wealth to make a difference?

> *The origins of the social component in corporate behavior can be traced back to the ancient Roman Laws and can be seen in entities such as asylums, homes for the poor and old, hospitals and orphanages. This notion of corporations as social enterprises was carried on with the English Law during the Middle Ages in academic, municipal and religious institutions. Later, it expanded into the sixteenth and seventeenth centuries with the influence of the English Crown, which saw corporations as an instrument for social development (Chaffee 2017). In the following centuries, with the expansion of the English Empire and the conquering of new lands, the English Crown exported its corporate law to its American colonies where corporations played a social function to a certain extent.* Extracted June 8, 2021, from, International Journal of Corporate Social Responsibility, *A literature review of the history and evolution of corporate social responsibility*, by Mauricio Andrés Latapí Agudelo, Lára Jóhannsdóttir & Brynhildur Davídsdóttir This section based on article by Chaffee, E. C. (2017). *The origins*

of corporate social responsibility. University of Cincinnati Law Review, 85, 347–373.

The health of any society's core is always based on sharing by choice, and as mentioned previously, when voluntary, great advancements can occur as our past golden ages are a testimony to.

> *"It is interesting that our personal use of virtue very much reflects the ups and downs of human civilization. During golden ages, integrity, morality, principles, and self-sacrifice were at their highest. Citizens gave of themselves to make their families, communities, and states or nations better."* Source; *Superstition to Maturity, The Evolution of Religion*, Raymond Chladny, Fiction Publishing, Inc. 2013

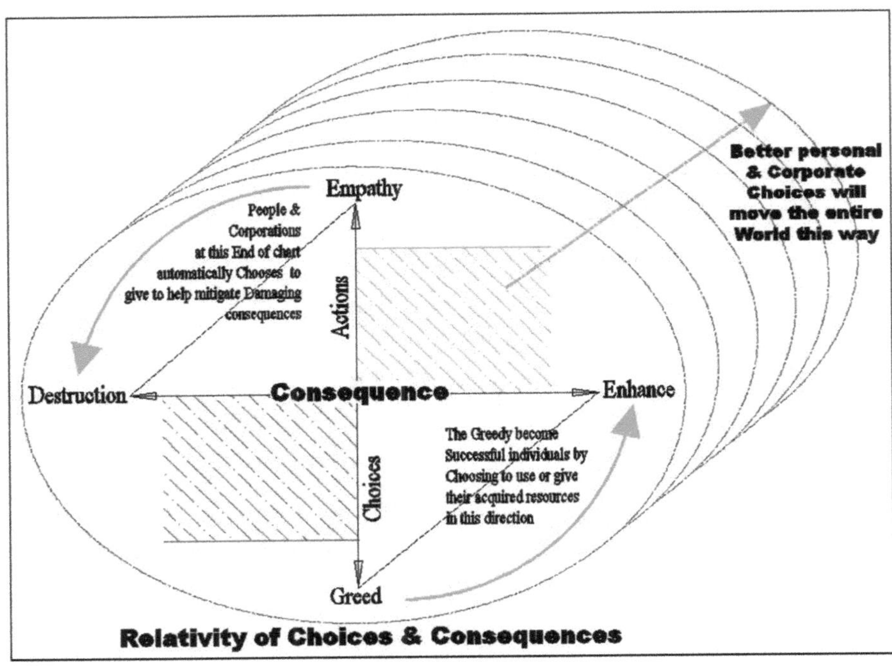

The above chart shows the consequences of the choices we make. Making money is not dirty or greedy, as long as our business culture nudges those who excel in gaining material rewards from their industry or service to give some back. These give-backs could be to improve the environment, eradicate disease, build institutions of higher learning, and help families, friends, and, of course, strangers less fortunate, with so many more possible solutions.

It cannot be over-emphasized that greed and lust for power are always the outcomes of an individual's choice, whether hiding inside a committee or just you; it's one's person's poor resolve . . . unprincipled, collapsing the pillars of virtue and always causes someone else, or something to suffer.

9

Can Socialism or Communism Be Ethical?

The Ethical Arrangement of society and the Economy- Society can be arranged along moral lines. The implications of a moral arrangement of society require the individual to conform their interest to the needs of society. An ethically arranged society and economy naturally lead to socialism. Socialism is by definition, the promotion of social good over all things. The Ethical Socialist will say "If it is possible to have a moral society without socialism, we would promote the moral society. But we do not think it is possible." Source; *Ethical Socialism*, Particracy, Wikipedia

The above justification is very cynical and leans heavily toward the belief that we are inwardly evil and, therefore, we need a government caretaker for morality. But in the big picture, which of these two options, *ethical socialism* or a *moral society without socialism*, does the most damage? As evident today, we see the main problem of a *moral society without socialism* is always a few people taking shortcuts within the free market for greed and power with little to no consequence. But is *ethical socialism* possible?

The socialists dream: "Every day I wake up with no worries about food, shelter, medicine, education, or clothes. I have a good government that looks after me and takes care of all my needs and troubles."

Is this sustainable? Can this really work, even under ethically intended and competent governance?

When placing this lofty dream into the relationships between ideals, virtue, and principle, we see both communism and socialism held the ideals of equality for all. It looks and sounds amazing, a life of minimum toil, never being in need or want.

Founded on the ideal by Karl Marx, communism has no free market, with the government controlling all industry. It is supposed to equalize all incomes without democracy and little liberty. It is completely top-down flow of everything. Even the government leaders must be changed by revolution rather than elections. Communism is the voice of the community (government in reality) and not the voice of the individual. By its very nature, this ideal is not sustainable as it compromises two very important virtues of justice and freedom.

Looking at historic attempts in communism, we see it not only compromises the above virtues but also in its own ideal of equality, with its leaders lavishing themselves in wealth while the masses live in attempts of economic equality, often resembling squalor with limited access to essential resources and services. Also, don't forget the hundred million deaths previously referenced.

In socialism, the government is elected, has a mix of public and private sectors, and does have a free market with high taxation to redistribute wealth in an attempt to equalize the extremes of wealth and poverty. This redistribution appears to be a noble thing as it works well for those who, due to physical or mental disability, cannot work, and also for those with never-ending medical costs. For those who are low to middle income, it looks very good, and for those earning more than the middle, socialism reduces their income through taxation in an attempt toward economic equality.

On the surface, this all sounds great, but this ideal ignores that inequality is found naturally in all things, and our societies are no different, as all people have different capacities, which lead to different social and economic standings. This falls in place with the previously provided definition of justice where, *"the just person wants their fair share, not more, not less."*... You get back what you put in. For example, would anyone be happy to work twice as hard as another able person and receive the same paycheck? Or someone who is a very talented musician and receives the same recognition and pay as another who is completely tone deaf? These are obvious injustices and, therefore, not compliant with virtues, undermining the stability of this ideal of equalization. One could argue the higher earners don't mind reducing their earnings to help those more in need. In the short term, this is noble, but over generations, other problems arise.

For example, the socialist approach leads to:

- Increased expectation for unearned resources;
- Diminished character development;
- Increased self-pity;
- Reduces personal accountability and self-reliance;
- Undermining working hard and ambition;
- Reduced risk-taking, affecting innovation, industry, and the arts;
- Devastating our personal and cultural growth; and
- Others will learn to "work the system," taking advantage of free opportunities under false pretense, basically stealing from the public trough.

Aside from the above damage, it would require a large tax base to pay for the large government to maintain its course before even helping anyone, and with stymied industry, where does the money come from to pay for itself without growing debt?

> *"Human beings are born with different capacities. If they are free, they are not equal. And if they are equal, they are not free."* Quote by Aleksandr Solzhenitsyn (1918-2008), Russian philosopher and historian.

Historically, we have seen similar ideals presented in numerous cults, where equality is confused with sameness, even requiring followers to have the same haircuts and clothes. The current "cancel culture" is very similar to these forced sameness movements by focusing on our historical, biological, and societal diversities, including our past, our thought, gender, ethnicity, work ethic, or given capacities. From a humorous perspective, maybe this movement will cancel the good-looking people used on TV and movies because their looks discriminate against the not-so-good-looking. Sadly, there is already discussion about eliminating gifted educational programs from schools because it discriminates against those not so gifted. No one should be held back for being gifted. Like the "crabs in a barrel" metaphor, where crabs get pulled back in, losing their freedom just because they have the given means to be so. As previously mentioned, it's these gifts that lead to excesses, which are to be shared in healthy societies. Nipping these gifts in the bud of hope can only destroy any prosperous societal future.

Socialism cannot be ethical with its premise of wealth equalization, as it compromises the virtues of temperance, wisdom, justice, and fairness. To accomplish this would require the government to press diverse incomes through a singularity mold for sameness. This will lead to changes in attitudes, from pride and self-worth to "who cares," undermining the work ethic. This sameness ideal would require a top-down oppression, which is expensive, inefficient, and contrary to anything natural or virtuous. It would resemble the diagram of "fake stability" on page 12.

Per two quotes by Friedrich Hayek (1899-1992), 1974 Nobel Prize in Economic Sciences: *"Economic control is not merely control of a sector of human life which can be separated from the rest; it is the control for the means of all our ends,"* and *"A claim for equality of material position can be met only by a government with totalitarian powers."*

Also, should a business's earnings' combined taxes charged be greater than 50 percent, then, in fact, that entity no longer represents the private sector but is under the socialist government's employ, making the economic structure similar to communism.

> *"The rightful path to socialism, according to the ethical socialists, is not social revolution but the moral evolution of all mankind; socialism, in their view, is primarily and above all a system of ethical values—a moral ideal as attractive as it is unattainable."* Source; *Ethical Socialism,* The Free Dictionary,

The above reference identifies a double flaw of ethical socialism. First, it is impossible to be ethical when its very method of operation compromises so many virtues, and second, historically and today, socialist leaders always make "the rules for thee and not for me," undermining its core ideal of equality.

Socialism, by its very nature, is inefficient in management, product quality, wasteful, slow to innovate, and lacks accountability. Even if we raise the societal bar and call this ideal ethical socialism, these constraints and inefficiencies are still there, it is all just done inefficiently without justice, but with honesty, a contradiction from within itself. Historically and still today, top-heavy leadership structures cannot work from an internal engine as their very ideal contradicts other inner virtues, leading to compromised principles and their ultimate failure.

The real essence of the economic equality-ideal has nothing to do with money amounts or equalization. Rather, a society that allows equal and unobstructed opportunity for all to access rewards equal to the contributions made, independent of race, ethnicity, or gender.

> *"Only an irrational man would want the state to run his life for him rather than create secure conditions in which he can run his own life. Only an irrational agenda would deliberately undermine the citizen's growth to competence by having the state adopt him. Only irrational thinking would trade individual liberty for government coercion, sacrificing the pride of self-reliance for welfare dependency. Only a madman would look at a community of free people cooperating by choice and see a society of victims exploited by villains."* Source, The Liberal Mind; The Psychological Causes of Political Madness by Lyle H. Rossiter, Jr., MD

Diversity is the core of the natural world's strength and beauty. The economic equality ideal as described above reflects the virtues of justice, love, temperance, courage, patience, wisdom, and knowledge, making it very sustainable. The virtue that needs to be added to this list and essential to any civilization is charity. It's not a failing of the free market but rather that of a few who choose to be immoral participants.

Charity, if legislated, becomes a form of taxation. It can only be a personal choice, and so it allows some to go unchecked to gather more money and things, morphing their hordes into a distorted abomination that serves no purpose except to feed their narcissistic egos. These individuals are no longer part of the social mechanism, floating independently from it, free to take from it whatever and whenever they want, and leaving the poor with little choice but to rely on inefficient government social programs. This lack of charity certainly builds a sense of unrest and injustice with the less fortunate, feeding these unsustainable socialist movements. We need to dig deeper to solve these problems and not repeat proven failing ways.

> *"There can be no peace in the world unless there's justice, and there can be no justice without peace. I think in a sense these problems are inextricably bound together."* Martin Luther King Jr, *Newsmakers*, King Center Library and Archives, Atlanta, GA, July 10, 1965.

10

A Science Parallel with the Failings of Socialism

In the world of physics, unstable conditions are always in a higher state of energy and continually "seek" to move its components toward a more stable (lower energy) state, sometimes passively and other times with an explosion. For example, in geology, molecules have an affinity to find like or compatible molecules to form beautiful crystals, releasing energy as they find their stable geometry. All chemical reactions work the same way, and once they find a state of equilibrium, the condition is calm. When natural forces within any complex or system are allowed to behave as they were created, they always shift to their most stable state.

Like the chemistry example, human society, too, seeks to find its equilibrium of peace and functionality. Social economic ideas, when following virtues and using good principles, require the least amount of energy and are, therefore, more sustainable. It's always the flawed ideal that needs a power control from the top-down to try and hold its failings together. A self-checking, virtuous, and principled system runs efficiently with little need for regulation and meddling from above.

From my personal experience based on working in capitalist, socialist and communist countries it appears that socialism govenments begin when more than 25% of its population is working for the public sector. This is confirmed by the statistics of a few countries. The

European Union and Canada are considered capitalistic with some socialist leanings, reflected in the average 18 percent and 20.2 percent respectfully, while Finland, a Nordic welfare state is at 26.1 percent, socialist China at 28 percent and communist Russia at 40.6 percent. The USA is at 13.3 percent. Source: https://en.wikipedia.org/wiki/List_of_countries_by_public_sector_size.

For clarification, a Nordic welfare state, also known as the Nordic Model or the Scandinavian model includes Finland, Iceland, Norway, Denmark and Sweden. All approach social aid in similar ways with high levels of support paid for by income taxes around 50 percent. Source: https://www.investopedia.com/terms/n/nordic-model.asp.

In all countries, the private sector along with revenues from natural resources have to generate the money to pay all public sector employee costs, public facilities, equipment and importantly, the people unable to work due to disability. Large public sector employee percentages makes sustainability more difficult, opening the door for a crowding-out effect on the private sector and feeding a growing national debt. When governments expand, they require more money, interest rates usually go up, and private sector investments goes down.

According to *The Economic Times*, the definition of the crowding-out effect is "*a situation when increased interest rates lead to a reduction in private investment spending such that it dampens the initial increase of total investment spending is called crowding.*" Source: https://economictimes.indiatimes.com/definition/crowding-out-effect

The quotes below are taken from a portion of an article from the Fraser Institute, written by Livio Di Matteo, Professor of Economics at Lakehead University, shows this very condition happening in Canada.

Source: https://www.fraserinstitute.org/article/times-have-changed-public-sector-employment-on-the-rise-in-canada-especially-in-ontario

See below:

> *From 2003 to 2013, employment in Canada's public sector increased by 22.6 per cent, more than double the rate of increase in the private sector (10.7 per cent). During this period, public-sector employment grew at a faster rate than the private sector in all the provinces except, again, Newfoundland & Labrador.*
>
> *By a considerable margin, this phenomenon was most pronounced in Ontario. From 2003 to 2013, public sector employment growth in Ontario (27.6 per cent) dramatically outpaced private sector employment growth (5.6 per cent) by a whopping 22 percentage points. Interestingly, Ontario's 10-year increase in public sector employment coincides with a period of dramatic increases in provincial government spending, rising government debt, and sluggish economic growth.*
>
> *There are important adverse economic and fiscal implications that may result from growing public-sector employment. Empirical research points to a so-called "crowding-out" effect where employment through public-sector job creation is offset by a reduction in private sector employment elsewhere in the economy. This is a concern because it's the private sector—through investment and innovation—that ultimately generates the wealth and taxes needed to provide the public services that we all hold dear.*
>
> *If public-sector employment simply crowds out private-sector employment, this could leave unemployment rates either unchanged*

or possibly higher. International empirical research has found some evidence of this crowding-out effect.

This type of system, with such high government employment, is mathimatecally illogical and certainly not sustainable. In Canada about 9.2 percent of it's GDP comes from natural resources, with more than half from fossil fuels, a quarter from minerals/mining, and one-tenth from foresty.

Source; Statistics Canada, *Natural resource indicators*, Mar. 25, 2021

Who or what will make up this difference to pay for all of this when the fossil fuels are "canceled" and other nonrenewable resources along with their associated revenues run out?

Besides socialism being fiscally impossible, four other failings of are:

1. The super-rich are still there, breaking the equalization ideal;
2. The poor through welfare live with minimal resources for life;
3. Those working due to high taxation are left with limited free capital; and
4. The welfare-poor and many of the working people lacking free capital are unable to enter home ownership.

High taxation and ongoing inflation is leading to an economic stratification in the housing market, creating a "landlords and the serfs" condition, which contradicts the socialist's equalization dream.

"A serf is a person who is forced to work on a plot of land, especially during the medieval period when Europe practiced feudalism, when a few lords owned all the land and everyone else had to toil on it. . . . The Latin root of the word is servus, which literally means "slave," but serf and slave are not synonyms." Source: Vocabulary.com

In Vancouver, Canada, socialism and unabridged immigration has caused the basic suburban home's worth to be in the millions, totally unaffordable for most of the old family population. In speaking with working people, many have multiple jobs, are homeless, and sleeping in their vehicles or on the streets.

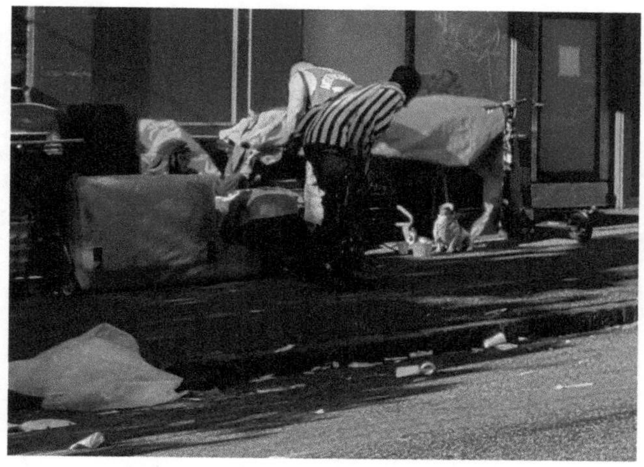

Homelessness in Vancouver, Canada. Photo by the author.

Other Canadian cities and California are in the same state. For most in Europe, the "landlord and serf" condition has long been an accepted birth condition. It's a form of discrimination to most of the population except for those born into houses, money, rich domestic corporations or the rich from other countries. In the big picture, this is not a stable state of equilibrium.

The average house in Vancouver, Canada, sells for 1.175 million dollars, most of which are in suburbia.

Source; *Average House Price in Vancouver,* The Canadian Magazine of Immigration, August 26, 2021.

Here is an extreme example of a small home for sale on a 0.14 acre lot.

407 W 43RD AVENUE
$9,800,000
OAKRIDGE VW VANCOUVER V5Y 2T9
RESIDENTIAL DETACHED BEDS: 4 BATHS: 2.0 2,156 SQ. FT.
BUILT: 1949
Details Photos Map
Prime Oakridge development location!! Located 1/2 block east of Oakridge Shopping Centre this property is part of Cambie Corridor Development Plan.
General Info:
Property Type: Residential Detached
Status: Active
Prop. Type: Residential Detached
MLS® Num: R2526559

Sale of a Single Family Home. Image extracted from The Vancouver MLS Listings, June 11, 2021.

From an actual land developer's experience in Canada:

A construction company in partnership with a landowner wants to design-build thirty beautiful brownstone walkup houses. In this type of endeavor, there is always a risk factor of runaway construction inflation, market collapse, or rental vacancy, resulting in investment losses. Before proceeding, an estimate of the return from fair market sales, construction costs, paying the architect and engineers, and paying the permit fees and impact fees were subtracted to see what was left as a net income. From this remaining balance, the government, through capital gains and local taxes, will take 75 percent, and the landowner and design-build company are left to share the remaining 25 percent.

From another perspective, what if this project went ahead and failed, causing bankruptcy? Maybe a lawsuit is thrown on top, which is not uncommon. Are the federal and local governments going to share your burden? No, the governments simply say that it's your problem now. But when you succeed, the socialist-type government is there to take a lion's share. To put this situation into a clearer perspective, if this government "partner" was a real person, would you agree to such terms? If you did, you'd be considered a very poor business person. But with the government, we're just supposed to say, "OK, here you go."

In this real example, it made no sense to proceed, and this project was canceled, resulting in site workers, carpenters, roofers, painters, and so on not getting the work, resulting in less free capital for them and, increasing their government reliance, and the greedy government, instead of taking the fair share plus the should-have-been-workers job taxes going back to them, gets nothing. This is simple logic and math. There's a healthy balance, where risk is worth taking, with fair reward, and the economy can thrive. Socialism just cannot deliver this.

There's an adage about greed, "pigs get fed, and hogs get slaughtered." In this situation, the government, instead of taking a fair cut, becomes the hog, reducing the livelihood of many and increasing people's dependence.

One could argue, "Well that 75 percent goes to help the less fortunate." But see chapter 14 ("Our Tax Dollar") to understand what really happens. As an example, say you have four cows, and the government says you have too many, and with the same ratio as above, takes three cows from you. Based on government inefficiency and the internal self-feeding, they will eat approximately 2.4 cows and only distribute 0.6 of a cow to the people.

In the long term, who does this really help? Breaching so many virtues, failure is always the outcome. In any ism, when ethics are not possible due to compromised virtue, not surprisingly, it will begin to unravel.

> *"If Socialists understood economics, they wouldn't be Socialists."* Quote by Friedrich Hayek, Nobel Prize in Economic Sciences.

An unexpected relationship between socialism and religion is that most who support socialism ideologies are also anti-religious. One needs to ask the question, if you want to be independent of God and His rules, then why hand your choices and money over to a government, allowing it to be your lord? Many secularists believe religious beliefs are to be overcome by a "higher" societal phase toward a modern socialistic society, basically godless.

> *"Thus, it can be said that on average people with socialist political views are more inclined to hold negative views about religion, than people with other political views."* Source: Egbert Ribberink, Peter Achterberg, Dick Houtman. *Are all Socialists Anti-religious? Anti-religiosity and the Socialist Left in 21 Western European countries* (1990-2008). February, 2015

So, can it generally be said?

Minimal or no God + big government + less choice (regulation and taxation) = socialism?

Some God + small government + more choice (free market and less taxes) = capitalism?

For those closed to the supernatural, God is fictitious, created for religious control, giving socialists comfort with government reliance to keep us behaving "properly." What's forgotten is that the government is made by humans and run by humans. Historical testimony is clear that the greatest sources of injustice and evil have been from governments, either directly or through a special interest party. See the section, "What Is Government?"

11

Building a New Business

Most entrepreneurs are risk-takers by nature, or at minimum calculated visionaries with a clear plan of action to launch a new product or service to fill a gap in the industry. On a personal level, many entrepreneurs take big risks to leave stable jobs to throw their efforts (and sometimes their own money) into launching a business. For entrepreneurs, there is no guaranteed monthly income, no guarantee of success, and spending time with family and friends can be a challenge in the early days of launching a company. Source; What Risks Does an Entrepreneur Face? By Adam Hayes, Investopedia. June 13, 2021

11a). What It's Like to Build a Business under Capitalism

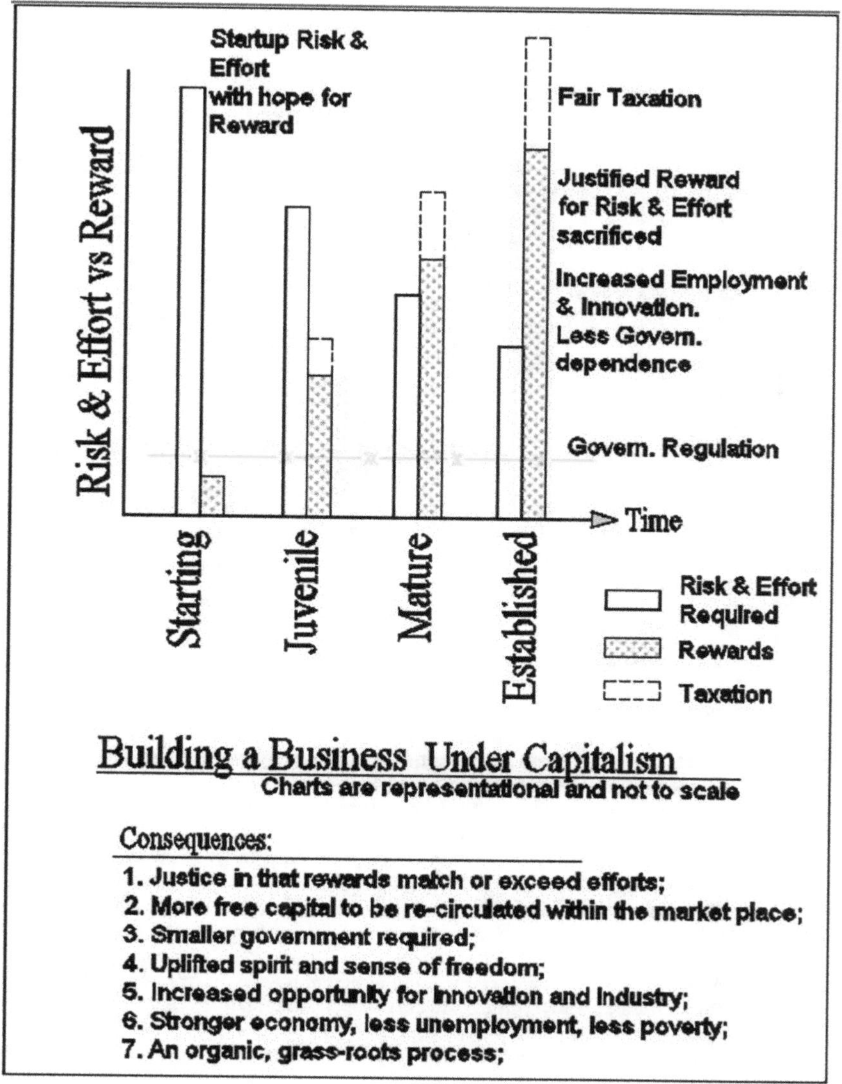
Startup Risk & Effort with hope for Reward
Fair Taxation
Justified Reward for Risk & Effort sacrificed
Increased Employment & Innovation. Less Govern. dependence
Govern. Regulation
Risk & Effort vs Reward
Time
Starting
Juvenile
Mature
Established
Risk & Effort Required
Rewards
Taxation
Building a Business Under Capitalism
Charts are representational and not to scale
Consequences:
1. Justice in that rewards match or exceed efforts;
2. More free capital to be re-circulated within the market place;
3. Smaller government required;
4. Uplifted spirit and sense of freedom;
5. Increased opportunity for innovation and industry;
6. Stronger economy, less unemployment, less poverty;
7. An organic, grass-roots process;

11b). What It's Like to Build a Business under Socialism

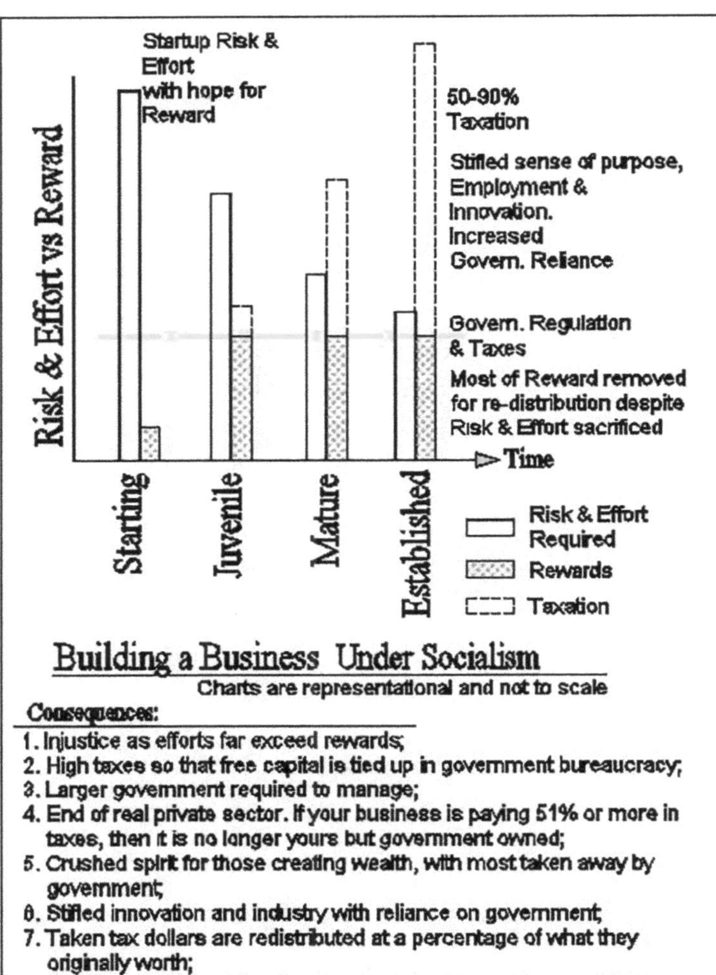

Startup Risk & Effort with hope for Reward
50-90% Taxation
Stifled sense of purpose, Employment & Innovation. Increased Govern. Reliance
Govern. Regulation & Taxes
Most of Reward removed for re-distribution despite Risk & Effort sacrificed
Risk & Effort vs Reward
Time
Starting
Juvenile
Mature
Established
Risk & Effort Required
Rewards
Taxation
Building a Business Under Socialism
Charts are representational and not to scale
Consequences:
1. Injustice as efforts far exceed rewards;
2. High taxes so that free capital is tied up in government bureaucracy;
3. Larger government required to manage;
4. End of real private sector. If your business is paying 51% or more in taxes, then it is no longer yours but government owned;
5. Crushed spirit for those creating wealth, with most taken away by government;
6. Stifled innovation and industry with reliance on government;
7. Taken tax dollars are redistributed at a percentage of what they originally worth;
8. Weaker economy, with unemployed and poor relying on government;
9. Those receiving government aid lose self-repsect as societal non-contributors;
10. A top heavy, over regulated self serving bureaucracy.
Government does not create wealth. It only redistributes and spends;

With the above, why would anyone want to invest so much risk and effort to start a business under a socialist system?

For anyone who is ill, disabled, or poor looking at the above two charts would prefer the socialist one, as they are normally not able to build a business and so turn to the government as their provider and shelter. Today, this is understood and even under a capitalist system government, social aid programs are provided. See the section on "Our Tax Dollar." However, government is slow to respond and has little reason to be creative, making government aid poor at best in both socialist and capitalist systems.

12

What Is a Corporation?

By definition, *"a corporation is a legal entity that is separate and distinct from its owners. Corporations enjoy most of the rights and responsibilities that individuals possess. An important element of a corporation is limited liability, which means that shareholders may take part in the profits through dividends and stock appreciation but are not personally liable for the company's debts. Corporations are not always for profit."* Source, Investopedia , by Will Kenton, *Corporation,* Feb 24, 2021

By giving the same rights a person can possess to a legal entity gives businesses much latitude to do great or terrible things, the results of which always come from individual choices (based on principles or lack thereof) and not a legal structure.

In business, there are corporates and companies, so what's the difference? According to DB (Difference Between.net), it is about suitability: *"Company is suitable form of business organization or legal structure for smaller businesses or entities; while corporate is more suitable for larger businesses or entities. Owners: The owners of a company are its members; while the owners of a corporate are its shareholders."*

Making a corporation a legal extension of a person is not so different than the development of a currency in place of trading goods or bartering. Both are constructs to yield economic simplification, fluidity, extended influence, efficiency, and power. With good principles, this works very well for society, but when choices are devoid of moral boundaries the results lead towards compromised worker and community safety, disaster and scandal.

Here are a few examples of some of the worst historic corporate acts, all being the result of corner-cutting or deception for greed:

1. The Enron scandal:

   "The situation started in early 2001, when analysts questioned the accounts presented in the company's previous annual report. These accounts used a variety of irregular procedures, which made it difficult to work out how the company was making money – despite it apparently having a foothold in energy, commodities and telecoms among other industries. The SEC began to investigate and discovered that Enron was hiding billions of dollars in liabilities through special-purpose entities (companies it controlled), which enabled it to appear profitable even though it was actually hemorrhaging cash. The company's share price fell from $90.56 to under a dollar as the crisis unfolded, with Enron forced to file for what was then the biggest chapter-11 bankruptcy in history." Source: https://www.ig.com/en/news-and-trade-ideas/top-10-biggest-corporate-scandals-and-how-they-affected-share-pr-181101#enron

2. The Volkswagen (VW) emissions scandal:

   Also known as "emissionsgate" and "dieselgate" – started in September 2015, when the US Environmental Protection Agency (EPA) announced that it believed VW had cheated emissions tests. It turned out that the company had been fitting what some industry commentators described as "defeat devices" to its diesel cars, which included software that would detect when the cars were undergoing laboratory testing and turn on controls to reduce nitrogen emissions. The cars would then appear to comply with the agency's standards but, in some cases, were actually emitting up to 40 times the nitrogen dioxide limit when driving on the road. This discovery led to investigations worldwide, with some estimates suggesting the scandal affected up to 11 million cars. Source: https://www.ig.com/en/news-and-trade-ideas/top-10-biggest-corporate-scandals-and-how-they-affected-share-pr-181101#enron

3. BP scandal:

> *"On April 20, 2010, a BP's Deepwater Horizon oil rig exploded, causing what has been called the worst environmental disaster in U.S. history and taking the lives of 11 rig workers. For 87 straight days, oil and methane gas spewed from an uncapped wellhead, 1 mile below the surface of the ocean. The federal government estimated 4.2 million barrels of oil spilled into the Gulf of Mexico."* Source, Penn State , The Arthur W. Page Center / Public Relations Ethics, extracted September 19, 2021.

The effects were devastating for the local ecosystem, wildlife, and locals, and BP has been forced to pay billions of dollars in compensation since the crisis. Today, after storms over the Gulf of Mexico, tar-like substances still wash up on the beaches. Many tons of sunken petroleum and disbursement agents still sit at the bottom for shellfish and crustaceans to eat, and then are harvested for public consumption. Wild life officers have secretly admitted to have found shrimp with three eyes and snook fish with two stripes instead of one.

4. The chemical poisoning from PFAS and PFOA (Fluoropolymers–Teflon):

During their mass production days of Teflon in the late 1900s to around 2015, these chemicals contaminated the drinking water of

70,000 people in West Virginia, causing illness, loss of life, and rendered our entire planet damaged indefinitely.

> *Scientists have confirmed links between PFOA exposure and a variety of serious diseases, including kidney cancer, testicular cancer, ulcerative colitis, thyroid disease, and pregnancy-induced hypertension. And more recent studies are now raising concerns that some of these forever chemicals may negatively impact our endocrine system, our fertility, and our immune system – and possibly even the efficacy of vaccines.* Source: The Guardian,

> *"The poison found in everyone, even unborn babies – and who is responsible for it,"* by Rob Bilott, 17 Dec 2020 06.16 EST

> *"Robin Andrews of Pedricktown, New Jersey, has been fighting an autoimmune disease and thyroid condition for the past three years, suffering severe dental problems, hair loss and other symptoms. All, she believes, are the result of exposure to drinking water tainted by a group of chemicals called PFAS, used widely for decades in products like Teflon pans, stain-resistant carpets, even cosmetics."* Source: NBC News, Gretchen Morgenson, March 1, 2020, 6:10 AM EST

5. The Titanic:

> *"The largest ocean liner in service at the time, Titanic had an estimated 2,224 people on board when she struck an iceberg at around 23:40 on Sunday, 14 April 1912. Her sinking two hours and forty minutes later at 02:20 on Monday, 15 April, resulted in the deaths of more than 1,500 people, making it one of the deadliest peacetime maritime disasters in history."* Source, Wikipedia, extracted June 12, 2021

A tragic accident, the result of the ship going too fast; some theorists believe White Star Line Owner was trying to set a new trans-Atlantic record, and others believe there was a coal fire threatening the ship while they attempted a full-speed crossing, leading to the fatal collision.

Source, History.com, updated: April 9, 2021

6. Great Molasses Flood;

> *"On the afternoon of January 15, 1919, a giant tank of molasses burst open in Boston's North End. More than two million gallons of thick liquid poured out like a tsunami wave, reaching speeds of up to 35 miles per hour. The molasses flooded streets, crushed buildings and trapped horses in an event that ultimately killed 21 people and injured 150 more. The smell of molasses lingered for decades."* Source, Emily Sohn, *Why the Great Molasses Flood Was So Deadly* Jan 15, 2019

The rupture was the result of poor design and neglect, making the accident more reckless and horrific.

There are so many stories similar to these throughout history. It seems all these disaster-causing corporations always put profit above service. It's, once again, greed; a lack of cooperation, whether it is a single individual or one hiding inside an entity; one person makes the good or bad choice and if the board is complicit, they, too, must be recognized as a criminal or as a hero. This is social justice.

12a). The Need for Corporate Reform:

Most of our corporate world cuts corners to some measure, every day within a culture affecting both their shares, employees' lives, and our environment. For example, when the shareholders' main interest is profit, it separates them from the business's service purpose of what it is supposed to provide. Making profit more important than providing needed products and services is a breach of societal trust, creating the same potential for new greedy disasters and scandals. To reduce the impact of greed motives, shareholders who are purely involved for money-in and profits-out, with no other internal role to improve the products or services, should have very little importance in its running. (See section on Shareholder Primacy).

A simple shortsighted example regarding corporations and employee treatment has to do with days of rest. Every nation has its days of national recognition in the form of a holiday. The USA created one of these national holidays for almost every month, yet if you're in the private sector, most have to go to work or face the threat of termination.

Choosing to place corporate interests above national holidays and the employees' quality of life is a form of greed and poor management. As a former employer and observing the paid holidays for my employees, it turned out to be very productive. Unrested employees with less time with family lead to many other problems, such as unhappiness, divorces, family violence, and stress-related illness, all leading to reduced productivity and, in the extreme, the need for government intervention.

In reality, to have your staff observe the holiday with pay increases your businesses' productivity and increases human happiness. We, as humans, are not machines, and if corporations won't step up, then some regulation is required; for example, if you want your Monday-to-Friday employees to work on a national holiday, they must be paid double time. Otherwise, these holidays are nothing but tokenism. It's all appearances and no substance.

Another corporate step-up besides these recognized national holidays is for new hired employers, after a minimum six-month probation period, to be given at least three weeks paid holidays per year, with opportunity to expand this time frame. It sounds costly, but when they come back rested, happy, and more productive, it is all a part of ethically capitalizing on your staff by adding to their happiness and increasing production with a bi-product of more profit.

> *"The research shows that far from being a brake on performance, that vacations actually increase productivity. Humans are simply more productive when rested. Researcher Mark Rosekind of Alertness Solutions found that the respite effect of a vacation can increase performance by 80%."* Source: Joe Robinson, *Increase Productivity, Take a Vacation,* Jul. 7, 2016

Ancient slave owners learned early that tired workers with malnutrition get far less done.

Employers cutting corners regarding their employees is not so different than the molasses disaster company not spending a little extra for the safety of the town. Shortcuts to save a buck always lead to long-term problems, as cutting days of rest can lead to mistrust, anger, and sabotage in the workplace. Also, what is happening at home that the police or social services have to pick up? None of this is free. Our taxation pays for it.

The USA mass shootings are usually from an individual's underlying unhappiness. Many USA employees have such limited time with their children due to many working multiple jobs. Kids are often left unattended away from Mom or Dad. This limited family time and the stresses they have to deal with can lead to crime or kids joining gangs as a quick fix, always with no happy ending.

We need to nurture a new business culture of cooperative worker-management-ownership relations, structured with an attitude of placing human service first and making money second. At first, this sounds like the antithesis of business, but in reality, your product or service becomes better because the service motive will challenge the greed "demon" from entering your industry. This is how ethical capitalism is supposed to work in a eudaimonic way.

Perhaps employers in large companies can give additional help to middle class workers through internal practices of improved human relations departments, which include the employee's home front. Say an employee's wife is home ill, can't work, and this is impacting the family's quality of life, instead of the family asking for help from the government through welfare programs, the employers can help by making a societal contribution through their own business culture and receive a tax credit. Social aid is the largest budget from taxation in the US and pays back very little of the tax dollar to those in need (see "Our Tax Dollar"). In the long run, grassroots "self-check" systems, organic in nature, are more efficient and cost less.

However a seeming paradox in helping employees is in regards to minimum wages. According to many economists, higher minimum wages simply lead to higher unemployment, causing more damage than good. Without starter jobs, what's the point of improving oneself, to learn simple skills and understanding how a free market is open to anything you want to do or be?

> *"The single largest problem with increases to the minimum wage is that they result in higher unemployment for low-skilled workers and young people. ... Research also indicates that employers often respond to increased minimum wages by reducing other benefits and on-the-job training."* Source; Fraser Institute, Sylvia LeRoy and Niels Veldhuis, *Does the minimum wage need to be raised?*

No: An increase hurts those it is meant to help, Appeared in the Vancouver Sun, June 2008.

Regardless of minimum wage arguments, corporations that mistreat their staff or planet are not capitalists but simply greedy, short-minded, and less sustainable. A real capitalist fully capitalizes on their resources by protecting and advancing them through ethical behavior, giving incentive to those who wish to work with the door wide open on how far their employees wish to go, and allowing success or failure to be based on one's own given capacities and the efforts made.

Ethisphere, an organization that rigorously rates businesses on five categories related to ethics, governance, responsibility, reputation, and company culture, has proven better behavior leads to better profits/capitalization identified by these findings. *"Companies listed on the 'World's Most Ethical Companies'* ranking outperform large-cap sector over five years by 14.4% and over three years by 10.5%." Source: EHS Today, *Being Ethical Has Its Perks: World's Most Ethical Companies,* March 4, 2019

13

What Is Government?

According to Dictionary.com, it is defined as *"The political direction and control exercised over the actions of the members, citizens, or inhabitants of communities, societies, and states; direction of the affairs of a state, community, etc.; political administration: Government is necessary to the existence of civilized society."* Source: www.dictionary.com/browse/government

Government is needed to ensure through regulation at least minimum standards are met for human and environmental protection, that we can trust in the products and services we are receiving, and to administer justice.

This is an essential trust relationship, which requires confidence that the other party will do what they are supposed to or expected to do. But where did the belief of government as honest, competent, and being on our side, yet see the private sector as greedy, corrupt, and against our personal interests come from? Who is the government, and why are so many of us quick to trust them to solve our societal problems?

Governments have been with us as long as history has records; they are engrained into all of us, plus government is physically there. Some see all corporations as self-serving and for the unbelieving, God is the unknowable, making God-trust much harder and possibly leading seculars to accept comfort and faith in their government above all else.

Trusting is a peaceful feeling. Without trust, we expend so much energy worrying, double-checking cooperation-compromised and choices, uncertain, making freedom impossible. So a trusting person must still act despite the possibility of nonperformance of an agreement or promise. However, trust can't just be given; it must be earned based on the character of the other party.

History remembers many greedy and destructive individuals and corporations. But history also shows governments have been villains on a much larger scale as they can affect entire nations. Here are some examples:

From 2017 to 2021, the Army Corps of Engineers were knowingly poisoning the people living along the Florida Indian River lagoon with water discharges laden with algal blooms one hundred times more toxic than what the EPA considers safe for human contact. Originally, no warnings were given of the toxic dangers to the residents until there was an increase in brain disease, sickness, and death of humans and wildlife, leading to a large public outcry. These nasty toxins were both water and airborne. These intentional acts are nothing short of domestic terrorism perpetrated by government officials, none of which were held accountable.

Source: The Author and his community were directly affected by this and active to rectify it as well.

Canadian Government: The Sexual Sterilization Act, created in 1928 and ran to 1972, with sterilizations, both compulsory and optional, performed on nearly 3000 "unfit" individuals of varying ages and ethnicities. Source; *Compulsory sterilization in Canada,* Wikipedia

Canadian Government & Residential Schools, run from 1883 to 1996:

But until 1883, Canada did not have a residential school system. Rather, it had individual church-led initiatives to which the federal government provided grants. Based on these pre-Confederation religious boarding schools, the government was to seek partnerships with representatives of the Anglican, Roman Catholic, Presbyterian, and other churches to operate the schools and to carry out this mission for the state. Religious instruction and discipline became the primary tool to "civilize" indigenous people and prepare them for life as mainstream European-Canadians. Source: Facing History & Ourselves, *Stolen Lives: The Indigenous Peoples of Canada and the Indian Residential Schools.*

In the spring of 2021, hundreds of unmarked graves were found of indigenous children around several of these schools, creating a huge scandal. Having personally met many victims of these schools, stories included children being taken from their parents without options, forced to surrender their language and culture, and sexually abused through pedophilia and rape. It reminded me of *Roots,* the mini-series with Kunta Kinte, which brings up slavery, another government atrocity, and for brevity, not expanded on here.

There are countless examples of government atrocities similar to the above, and here are a few historic extremes:

Adolf Hitler: 6 million Jews and 10 million or more of Russians and others were killed. Besides these deaths, German pharmaceutical companies tested drugs on camp prisoners; other companies built the crematoria. As prisoners entered the death camps, they surrendered all personal property. Each of us should further explore details so this is never to be forgotten. Source; Wikipedia, *The Holocaust.* Extracted, July 19, 2021.

Pol Pot: Cambodian genocide he committed through the Khmer Rouge, a radical communist movement that ruled Cambodia from 1975 to 1979 and systematically persecuted and killed Cambodians, which they saw as enemies. *"The genocide, coupled with malnutrition and poor medical care, killed between 1.5 and 2 million people, approximately a quarter of Cambodia's population."* Source; Cambodian genocide, Wikipedia, June 30 2021

Atomic Bomb Drops: *"The United States detonated two nuclear weapons over the Japanese cities of Hiroshima and Nagasaki on 6 and 9 August 1945, respectively. The two bombings killed between 129,000 and 226,000 people, most of whom were civilians, and remain the only use of nuclear weapons in armed conflict."* Source; *Atomic bombings of Hiroshima and Nagasaki*, Wikipedia, June 30 2021.

There is much argument on whether Truman had other options to have prevented this mass killing of civilians to end WWII. It is an interesting study to explore but beyond the scope here.

Weaponized Insects: Known as *"Entomological warfare (EW) is a type of biological warfare that uses insects to interrupt supply lines by damaging crops, or direct harm to enemy combatants and civilian populations. There have been several programs which have attempted to institute this methodology; however, there has been limited application of entomological warfare against military or civilian targets."* This type of warfare is extreme, as it hits everyone, including our natural ecosystems, not just the military. It was used by Japan against China and was considered by the Soviet Union, United States, Germany, and Canada all during WWII and the Cold War. *Entomological warfare*, Wikipedia. Extracted August 21, 2021

In these extremes, it seems that governments do not behave as individuals but rather as mobs. The ringleaders have a face, and the rest blend into a veil of bureaucracy, working largely without repercussions for themselves. As in these few examples, they hide behind an "iron fist" legislature/policy/propaganda, not founded on principle or virtue. These and many other historic disaster-governments always put power and control above serving their citizens.

To reduce the chance for this to happen again, the government needs to be kept small. Smaller governments are easier to watch and, by their scale, are more transparent. Individuals can be called out and held accountable for both good and bad behavior. The same can be said about large corporations. Perhaps breaking them up into smaller competitive industries is more effective for human service and supply as well.

The Peruvian economist, Hermando De Soto Polar (1941–), is a great proponent to this philosophy.

> *De Soto was a member of the ILD (Institute for Liberty and Democracy) and became a known player and made changes in Peru's economic systems that allowed the property system of Peru to operate in plain sight as opposed to the black market it had operated in previously. The changes implement allowed many firms to prosper, which can be attributed to the removed bureaucratic red tape, which previously meant that starting a new business would take a lot of time and be costly. The changes made were so significant that the guerrilla movement known as the Shining Path were becoming deprived, which resulted in a terrorist attack. Following the work carried out in Peru during the 1980s heads of state from all over the world have sought the services of the ILD, predominantly with a focus on improving the economic infrastructure. A series of reform programs designed by the ILD has become the inspiration of major initiatives in companies such as Egypt, Honduras and Tanzania. The focus of the ILD has also allowed for more*

recognition of what the less fortunate and poor have to face on a daily basis. Sources: https://www.leadersforbusiness.com/hernando-de-soto-polar/

Historically and today, government always looks to increase their budgets with these costs being imposed on the people. In the private sector, the capable move up; in government, this process, though recognized, is mottled with those incompetent being promoted more through seniority rather than for ability.

If you are very efficient at your job in the government, you're often asked to slow down. In the private sector, free market, you are encouraged to keep doing better. So how can the government be better for employee self-esteem or compete with the private sector toward a stronger national economy?

Having worked for and with many governments, I've seen that most are competent individuals; some that I have spoken with are performing doubled-up jobs due to poor upper management.

So why do people want to become government workers?

a) They want security in the workplace, which they see the government as that, incarnate. However, it must be remembered that it's the private sector that makes the money to pay these "secure" government jobs. Government is mostly on the service end and does not directly add wealth to the economy. Even the payroll taxes government workers pay back were originally taken from the earnings of the working private sector.

b) They want to minimize stress with most working nine to five and a guaranteed pension at the end of their term. They seek the merry-go-round, wanting more of the same, and avoiding the roller coaster. They see this as a happy context and often work hard to grow the government larger with increased regulation requiring new departments to make a larger insulated security nest for themselves.

c) Opportunities for promotion with reduced competition. New government positions for workers are often done through internal postings, exempt from private sector applications, keeping it in the "family." Sadly, the result is fewer outside ideas and talent, promoting more of the same with limited innovation.

Government failure – When public sector intervention leads to inefficiency

Caused by:

- **Lack of incentives.** Public sector workers less likely to be paid for performance / profit targets.
- **Levels of bureaucracy.** Governments tend to have more layers of administration and planning.
- **Political interference.** Decisions made for short-term political gain – rather than sound economics, e.g. keep on unproductive workers.
- **No consistency.** Change of government often leads to change of approach and new political initiatives.
- **Moral hazard** – Government can act lender of last resort - this may encourage banks to take risks knowing they will be bailed out.
- **Regulatory capture** – When government agencies become too friendly with business/groups they are trying to regulate.
- **Unintended consequences.** Policies to reduce relative poverty 'means-tested benefits' can create 'welfare dependency.

www.economicshelp.org

Source: https://www.economicshelp.org/microessays/market-failure/government-failure/ Extracted May 31, 2021

In an ideal world, the government would be successful in regulating firms, labor markets and running public industries. However, government intervention is prone to government failure and an inefficient allocation of resources. For example, labor market regulations such as high minimum wages or maximum working week could lead to unemployment and a lack of flexibility which firms need to deal with a sudden increase in demand. If firms are highly regulated, it is an extra cost which may discourage investment and lead to lower economic growth. Source: https://www.economicshelp.org/blog/147271/economics/pros-and-cons-of-socialism/ Extracted June 3, 2021

The extremes of government regulation lead people to desperation, even risking their lives for freedom. This homemade craft was found on Jensen Beach, Florida, on October 03, 2021. And it most likely came from Cuba or Haiti. It was uncertain if anyone survived.

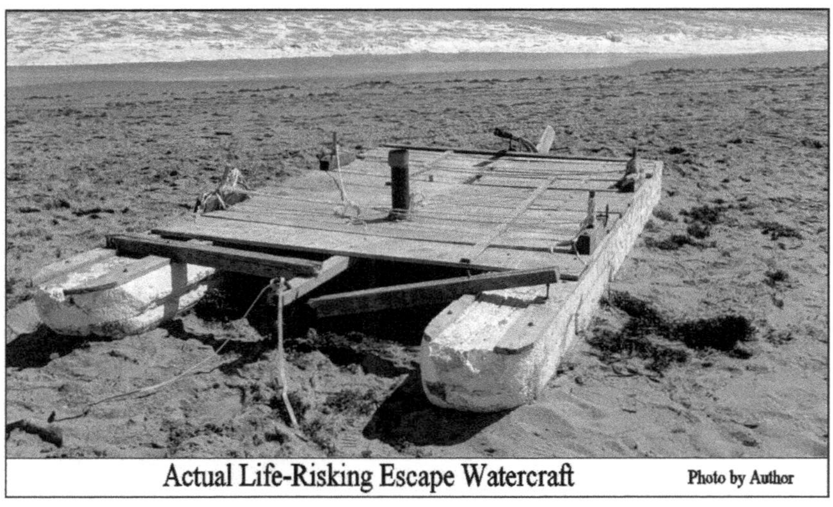

Actual Life-Risking Escape Watercraft Photo by Author

Despite this negativity, as mentioned, the government is essential for setting regulations to protect human rights, preserving environment, culture, and quality of life, based on research and democracy, and then to ensure those standards are met, the private sector is always more efficient and less costly to run, and as such, the government should not compete with the private sector. Remember, added costs to industry from bureaucratic regulation are always passed onto the consumer.

14

Our Tax Dollar

Where does the government get its tax dollars from, and where does it go? Due to covid (2019–2022), with incentive payments in the trillions, the national debt and interest portion will be much higher than shown on these two USA-based pre-covid charts below.

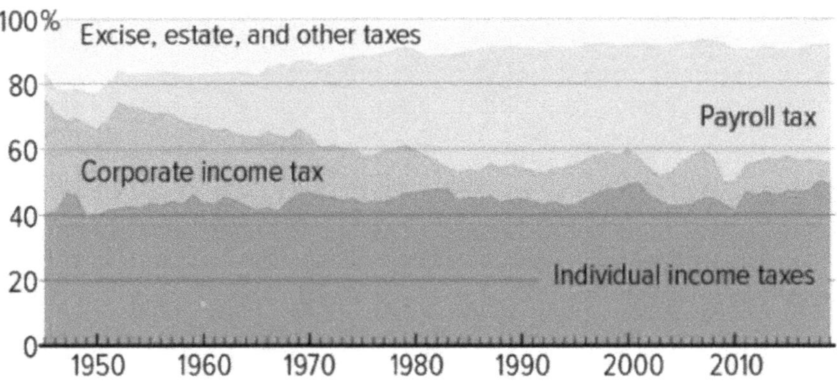

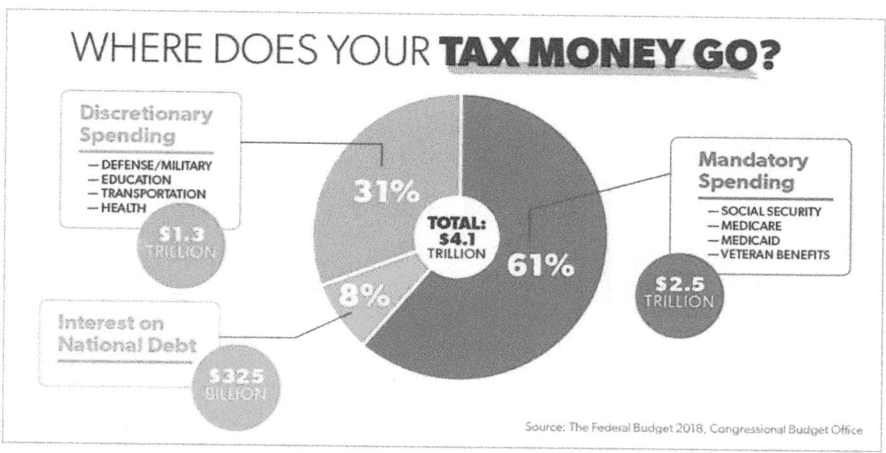

Money goes in, and a lot less comes out.

The Canadian Taxpayers Federation analysis, based on six years of financial statements, revealed that the Canadian government has spent considerably more than it has taken in, and again, this is before the covid bail-out checks.

> *"A preliminary financial report of this fiscal year — from April 1, 2018, to March 31, 2019 — shows the Liberal government is on pace to post a budgetary deficit of about $15 billion, yet another double-digit billion-dollar shortfall in the government's budget after being $19 billion in the red the previous fiscal year."* Source; Toronto.com, by Sheila Wang, *How does the Canadian government spend your tax dollars?*, June 13, 2021

For the USA, according to Randy Simmons, a senior fellow at the Independent Institute and professor of economics at Utah State University, stated in an article published in PERC on Wednesday, October 1, 2008, *"In the United States less than one quarter of every dollar spent on welfare makes it into the hands of the needy. The rest is consumed by people between the Congress and the intended recipient. Aid to Africans is even worse with fewer than 15 cents of every dollar finding its way to the poor."* Source: Property and Environment Research Center (PERC), *If You Really Want to Help the Poor, Remember Milton Friedman*, Volume 26, No.3, September 16, 2008.

So the USA government takes a dollar and delivers fifteen to twenty-five cents and with mediocre results for whatever is in need.

15

Fear for Control

"The whole aim of practical politics is to keep the populace alarmed (and hence clamorous to be led to safety) by menacing it with an endless series of hobgoblins, most of them imaginary." Quote by HL Mencken (07/12/1880-01/20/1956), an American scholar.

Most governments have used fear to maintain power, control, and taxation. Historically, fear through marshal law, later evolving to a more people-friendly leadership due to the repeating public rebellions, and later still, the fear method shifted toward demonizing the competing neighbors or nations.

John Adams, in *Thoughts on Government,* cynically wrote, *"Fear is the foundation of most governments."* Source: *Republican Government,* Chapter 4, Document 5, Apr. 1776.

Fear always makes people yield or pay more to the government to avert these fears, real or not. Economists can actually calculate tradeoff values from market context choices with the people's willingness to pay extra to reduce the risk of whatever the fear maybe. When used with people's death risks, it is called VSL, or Value of Statistical Life. In a real situation, it's a great tool, but in sinister hands, it can look very scientific to milk the population for ulterior motives.

"It is increasingly common to include estimates of value of statistical life (VSL) in analyses of proposed policies that affect people's

mortality risks. While such VSL estimates have often been derived using methods that, for example, compare wage differentials between risky and non-risky jobs, such methods may be inappropriate to assess the value of very different environmental, health and transport risks affecting the general population." Source; Organization for Economic Co-operation and Development (OECD), *Meta-analysis of Value of Statistical Life estimates*, extracted Sept. 17, 2021.

It is very difficult to know if we are on a path of truth or deception as convincing expert writings and lectures can be found on opposite ends of any issue. Skepticism of our own beliefs and what we are told is essential to remain closer to what is really true.

Today, with glimmerings of world peace, these previous fear methods are harder to use and, sadly, new, more insidious methods have been created, some by governments, others by yellow journalists, and others from political activists. Here are some fear examples:

1. Repetition of false narratives: Giving partial information, enough to sway the masses in an intended direction, resulting in the current journalist and news stations, calling each other "fake";
2. To speak freely: Repercussions or silencing by threats from groups with different opinions;
3. Third parties watching our own behavior: Orwell's "1984", with cameras everywhere;
4. Scientific information: For example, population growth, climate change, oceans rising;
5. Global pandemics: Dangerous or not, can be accidental or made, but will restrict personal freedoms; and
6. Violent protests: Expanded beyond what they originally stood for to feed a narrative.

The control comes in the form of violence, censorship, fines, job loss, imprisonment, taxation, or whatever is deemed appropriate by the advocates, government, journalists, or scientists.

These are all rife with much emotional contention, leading to some becoming weaponized.

Simply look at the impact and fear related to the covid pandemic. Government control was near martial law in many countries. Pharmaceutical companies and lobbyists took advantage while many small businesses disappeared and places of worship were shut down, leaving so many unanswered questions that even the scientists and doctors cannot agree. Much death with contradictory procedures, statistics, and unprecedented spending, the world will never be the same.

> *The various Covid-19 vaccines currently being distributed around the globe have the potential to end the worst pandemic in a century. They also will mean hundreds of billions dollars in sales for the pharmaceutical companies that make them. Despite being priced at less than $20 per dose, Pfizer (PFE) expects sales of the vaccine it developed with BioNTech (BNTX) to total about $15 billion by the end of this year, with a profit margin of nearly 30%.* Source; Chris Isidore, New York CNN Business, *Here's what Covid vaccines are worth to Big Pharma*, March 15, 2021.

16

Global Warming

Global warming has huge implications on economics, technology, societal structure, and the health of all species around the world.

We must be the shepherd of our earth, but the difficulty is to get the entire planet to join in, especially the highly populated cities and nations with minimal regard to stop the polluting and "clean up" their messes.

The nonprofit organization GlobalGiving lists the man-caused sources for climate change below.

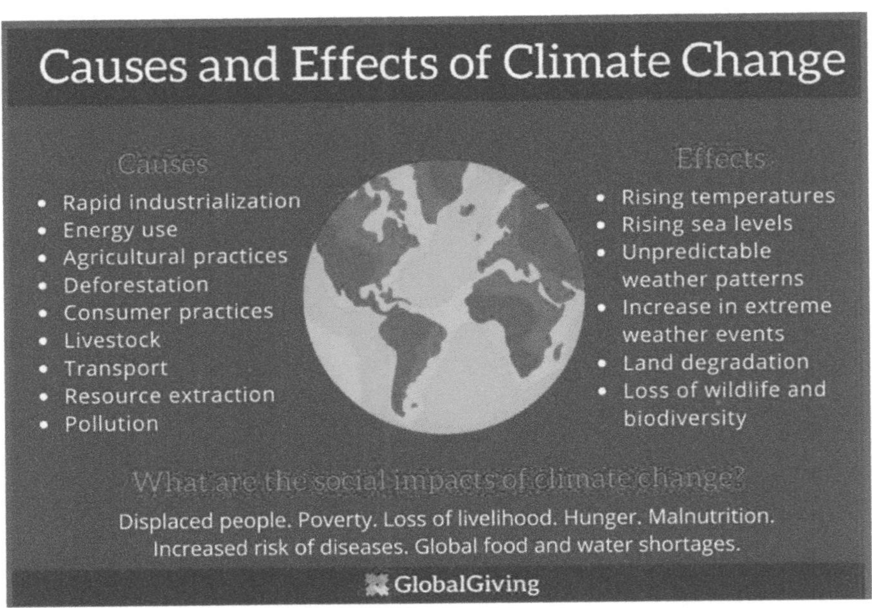

Causes and Effects of Climate Change
Causes
Rapid industrialization
Energy use
Agricultural practices
Deforestation
Consumer practices
Livestock
Transport
Resource extraction
Pollution
Effects
Rising temperatures
Rising sea levels
Unpredictable weather patterns
Increase in extreme weather events
Land degradation
Loss of wildlife and biodiversity
What are the social impacts of climate change?
Displaced people. Poverty. Loss of livelihood. Hunger. Malnutrition.
Increased risk of diseases. Global food and water shortages.
GlobalGiving

Besides these man-made factors, some natural ones affecting climate change are solar variations, the moon's gravitational forces, volcanoes, clouds, internal earth changes, ocean changes, and more. All of these affect the balance of heat-in versus heat-out from our planet, and today these are beyond our technical control.

Some believe the sun is the main cause of this warming trend, but the graph below shows the sun's irradiance went down between 2000 and 2008 while the earth's temperature continued warming by about 0.5 degrees Celsius, indicating there are other factors at play besides the sun.

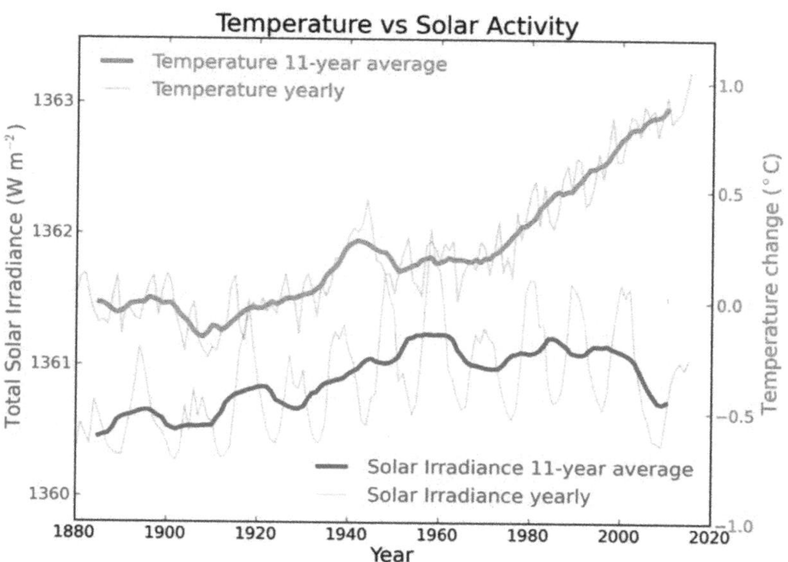

"Annual global temperature change (thin light red) with 11 year moving average of temperature (thick dark red). Temperature from NASA GISS. Annual Total Solar Irradiance (thin light blue) with 11 year moving average of TSI (thick dark blue). TSI from 1880 to 1978 from Krivova et al 2007. TSI from 1979 to 2015 from the

> *World Radiation Center."* Source: Skeptical Science, *Sun & climate: moving in opposite directions,*

Some believe volcanoes are a large climate changing factor for events like the Little Ice Age (AD 1645 and AD 1715), but based on NASA research, their impact pales in comparison to the human one. Today, it is believed the Little Ice Age was caused by our sun's Maunder Minimum.

> *By comparison, human activities emit a Mount St. Helens eruption of CO2 every 2.5 hours and a Mount Pinatubo eruption of CO2 twice daily. The largest possible eruptions come from super volcanoes like Yellowstone or Mount Toba (which erupt very rarely, about every 100,000-200,000 years or more), but the total annual CO2 emissions from human activities is like one or more Yellowstone-sized super eruptions going off every year. So, the human impacts are quite large compared to volcanoes.* Source; NASA, *Global Climate Change*. Extracted Sept. 17, 2021.

The majority of our atmospheric gases are oxygen and nitrogen, which are transparent to infrared light or energy reflecting back up from the earth's surface, but water vapor, carbon dioxide, methane, and other trace gases are opaque to them and get absorbed, reflecting some of their heat back to earth's surface, known as the "greenhouse effect." These gases occur from our carbon-based industrialization as well as naturally. Sadly, as the earth's temperatures increase, so does the release of water vapor from our oceans, adding to an accelerated greenhouse loop.

The warming increases seem to have started around 1975. What event(s) triggered this to begin then and not earlier? Was there a giant increase in automobile numbers and coal burning, or has the accumulation of pollution from the beginning of industrialization finally tipped the earth's stable state? There are probably scientific studies for these important questions, along with how much of this CO_2 is natural or from our industry; however, this goes far beyond the scope of this book and is something the reader is encouraged to explore.

The nonprofit GlobalGiving estimates it would take between $300 billion and $50 trillion to end global climate change over the next two decades. This huge disparity is because experts disagree on what is specifically required to stop the warming.

For those who reject climate change as man-made, they can say the reports by NASA, an arm of the government, are doctored as a fear mongering tactic and as skeptics are encouraged to explore other credible sources of research meanwhile the above disparity leaves a huge opening for the possible misuse of climate control narratives. We need to ensure our information is based on real science and not on motifs to keep the status quo regarding our ongoing polluting or allow governments to control the population through public hysteria.

Suggested solutions like the "green-new-deal" to combat global warming are very top-heavy with new government branches and massive tax increases, crushing economic growth. They are wasteful, inefficient, and not innovative. If these costs are collected by the government as another tax, will our dollars suffer the same inefficiency seen for social aid at 15–25 percent?

Also government-pushing electric cars look like a good solution, but where does the power to charge these cars comes from? According to the US Energy Information Administration in 2020, the sources were as follows: 60.3 percent fossil fuels, 19.7 percent nuclear plants, and 19.8 percent renewables sources. It's obvious that our power sources are the problem with the need for cleaner, renewable, and more robust power sources.

The pie chart below shows the causes for the CO_2 pollution. These emissions in each of these sectors stem from our modern technology, invented by industrialists and built by industry.

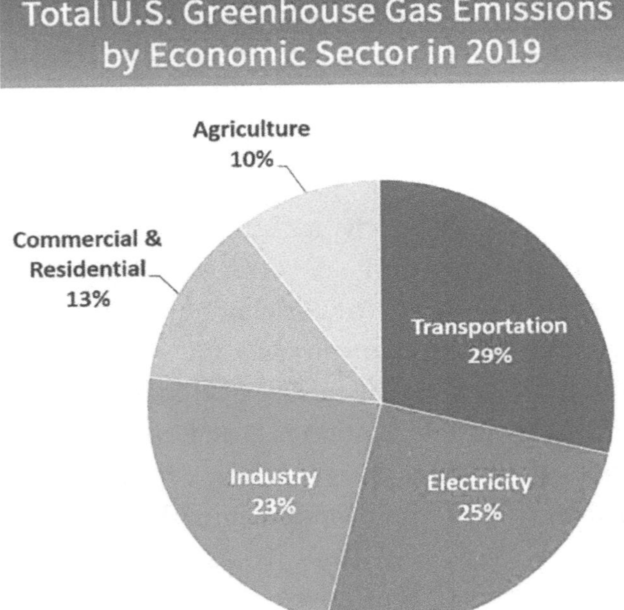

Source; United State Environment Protection Agency, Sources of Greenhouse Gas Emissions, extracted Sept. 19 2021

Increasing government spending to counter this suffers the same failings previously discussed. Within a free market, the industry sees this as a new business opportunity to seize and work toward CO_2 reduction/elimination. This process can be sped up with tighter government "clean" standards, codes, and new legislature to encourage the development of environmentally friendly innovation. This process has already begun with more stringent energy codes and standards for reduced emissions as indicated by the chart below.

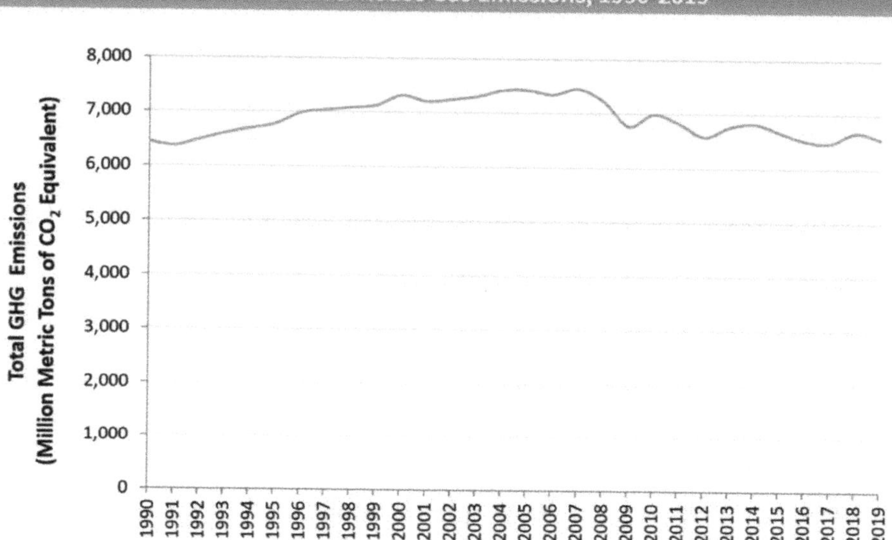

Source; United State Environment Protection Agency, Sources of Greenhouse Gas Emissions, extracted Sept. 19 2021

This is a healthy public-private relationship, where the government encourages the industry to be innovative rather than a stifling industry through taxation and regulation. It's metaphoric to a marriage between the government and industry. In a healthy marriage, the spouses live and work together based on virtue and trust, encouraging each to their best capacity. This is always more productive and certainly happier than one spouse using control and fear over the other.

While industry is cleaning up their messes, a possible intermediary solution instead of government spending is climate change insurance. We have hurricane and flood insurance, so why not for buildings in more risky areas like those on permafrost or flood areas pay more just as others do in higher risk areas for hurricanes, and so on? As referenced below, the insurance industry is very wealthy.

> *Total property/casualty cash and invested assets were $1.9 trillion in 2019, according to S&P Global Market Intelligence. Life/annuity cash and invested assets totaled $4.3 trillion in 2019; separate accounts assets and other investments totaled $2.8 trillion. The total of cash and invested assets for both sectors was $9.0 trillion. Most of these assets were in bonds (57 percent of property/casualty assets and 71 percent of life/annuity assets, excluding separate accounts).* Source: NAIC data, sourced from S&P Global Market Intelligence, Insurance Information Institute.

The reliance on a free market and the industry picking up the torch for this "world-saving" effort makes it so much more important for capitalism to be operating on its founded internal rules.

17

Ethical Capitalism: Toward Eudaimonia

> *"Capitalism is the root cause of a global increase in living standards on a scale unprecedented in human history before the emergence of the market economy. This has been verified by calculations from the economist J. Bradford DeLong from the University of California."* Source; Forbes, by Rainer Zitelmann, *Is the Gap Between The Rich And The Poor The Real Problem?* Aug 19, 2019

As mentioned in the prologue, those with limited economic knowledge think capitalism and greed are related and, certainly, they are not. Greed can be found in any human construct and is simply an individual's choice and not a product of any ism. Capitalism does not need the pre-fixes, such as real, quasi, ethical, moral, distributive, or so many others. From its earliest inception, it was created to be virtuous, ethical, distributive, and, in its highest form, is the only economic system we know that can reach eudaimonia.

> *While still far from a "free economy," China's newfound openness to free-market principles is correlated with the most substantial example of poverty reduction in the history of the world. Even if correlation does not always equal causation, that accomplishment is difficult to ignore. Granting people the freedom to voluntarily make mutually beneficial exchanges of goods and services has been the most effective anti-poverty solution to date. As more of the world*

> *allows the exercise of such freedom, expect poverty to decline even further.* Source; By Luka Ladan, *Capitalism Remains the Best Way to Combat Extreme Poverty*, June 14, 2019

So why is ethical capitalism the best hope for a state of eudaimonia . . . a healthy, happy, and prosperous human society?

As mentioned above, the pronoun "ethical" is not necessary to be associated with capitalism because, by its very nature, it is impossible to render exploitation and destruction, as these are seen as inefficiencies, a loss of capital and opportunity, poor management, incompetence, shortsightedness, or corruption. Its very name implies capitalizing on the resources available; anything else is its abandonment for greed or power lust.

It's amazing how a fair free market fulfills all our societal needs. Any missing service or product will be picked up by someone, and new advancements are always to be discovered to expand the free market opportunity. Going back to the current climate change issues, the free market will be quick to seize opportunity and find environmental solutions to slow the storm and contribute to the much-needed cleanup.

Capitalism's inherent structure/framework takes in rather than contradicts virtue and principle. It's the only economic-social structure we know that actually uplifts and feeds virtue and expands the door for principle and service. The best capitalists are those most virtuous and principled within their chosen mode of business operation and policy. The ideal under capitalism is freedom; the virtues it imbibes are courage, temperance, ambitiousness, creativity, friendliness, gentleness, generosity, magnificence, magnanimity, truthfulness, wittiness, justice/fairness, knowledge, intellect, and wisdom, all identified here by Aristotle. Notice that greed, control, and power-seeking are absent because these are not virtues but rather personal unprincipled choices external to any ism.

Skeptics would argue that capitalism today is the opposite of this, and for many of today's businesses, this is true. But with the real definition of capitalism, those bad businesses are simply immoral, the fruit of bad, unprincipled people running them and nothing to do with capitalism.

When a free market business is run with good principles, it will flourish on the inherent built-in virtues of capitalism. Imagine a principled business working under these virtues; people would be drawn to interact with it like moths around a light. The principle of service would be its motivation and profits its reward. Another skeptic could argue that socialism would work the same, but it can't as it breaks the virtues of justice, compromises courage, erodes ambitiousness, and reduces the need for intellect and wisdom due to third-party dependencies. It can't be over emphasized that:

1. Any ism (ideal) that contradicts virtues also contradicts the pillars of society and is simply not sustainable;
2. Greed can interfere with any ideal; and
3. Capitalism is the only ism that can function so perfectly with all of Aristotle's virtues, naturally flourishing internally and so requiring less regulation.

When solving mathematical problems, like isms, the simplest is usually the right one.

The beneficiaries are improved environment, employee happiness, social, artistic, and scientific advancement, capitalizing on the abundance of resources all around us, and yielding unlimited choices. Recognized as an important part of society, the successful would have more resources to give back to the less fortunate, reducing that burden from the government and the rest of the working population. If it doesn't operate this way, then it's not ethical and not capitalism. Measures to offset those individuals choosing non-participation are explored later.

18

Management of Our Resources

In a unified capitalist world, nations would investigate and identify all their resources. These economic resource sources can be broken into two main groups, each of which has numerous subgroups; however, for brevity, these subgroups are not listed here:

1. Capitalism and the human resource
2. Capitalism, our planet, and the universe

Instead of a haphazard free market, an intelligent manager would create a plan to ensure their resources are best used for their well-being and to ensure their enriched expanse and sustainability.

18a). Capitalism and the Management of the Human Resource:

> "*Train people well enough so they can leave. Treat them well enough so they don't want to.*" Quote by Sir Richard Branson, British business magnate and author.

A good management plan would be structured to motivate and maximize our free thoughts, creativity, and human opportunity, be it public, private, or religious, and reward both discovery and ethical/moral behavior. This should start on the community level by supporting education, arts, and healthy family activities.

Imagination with morality is the little bit of God in each of us, the thing our parents, philosophers, and spiritual advisers taught and hoped we would be. Imagination is our greatest resource. It created language, numbers, equations, arts, and music. It's the reason for our survival against the odds in our earliest beginnings. Today, we see corporate greed, religious dogma, government regulation/taxation tearing the hearts from innovative souls, hindering their personal dreams, and ideas, which could possibly lead to bigger things like environmental cleanup, off-grid power systems, or even antigravity motion, to name a few.

Capitalism, when working properly, is an ecosystem with morality. According to the Encyclopedia Britannica, an ecosystem is defined as *"the complex of living organisms, their physical environment, and all their interrelationships in a particular unit of space."* Source: https://www.britannica.com/science/ecosystem. Interestingly, there is no third party overseeing its functioning. Its diversity and interrelationships are what keeps it healthy and strong.

The word ecosystem includes eco, on which our economy is very much dependent. *"Our ecosystem, the earth, ultimately controls our economic systems because it provides us with what we need for our economies (and everything else) to actually exist. For example, we must have water, food, and goods that we then buy, sell, or trade with others in order to profit economically."* Source; LinkedIn, *What business ecosystem means and why it matters,* extracted June 14, 2021

For an economic free market to work like a natural ecosystem, all players would have to play fairly or be squeezed out by the ecosystem's inner natural works. The balance of all the interrelations and exchanges will not tolerate bad actors and protect the rest of us from them. However, in our economic system today, we see the natural or *the invisible hand* alone is unable to provide the moral/virtuous principles real capitalism requires to combat these narcissistic individuals.

According to OXFAM International, the wealthy corporations and super-rich are massively under taxed while essential public services, like healthcare and education, are underfunded. Obviously, corporations and individuals with large earnings need to start paying their share to counter the growing, justified, social unrest.

The typical approach is for the government to increase taxes to help the ill and poor. But as previously discussed, so much of the tax dollar collected goes into bureaucratic offices, supplies, and salaries instead of directly helping those who really need it.

Throughout history, those with the gold have always made the rules, "the golden rule." So expecting the rich to pay high taxes is unlikely to change for a very long time, as money is power. Perhaps an incentive would be to celebrate the corporations or the rich when they make real social contributions, as good citizens on a local and global platform rather than just giving them a tax deduction. Volunteering donations to help the less fortunate are always more palatable to anyone and can be encouraged through a second invisible hand discussed later.

Currently, besides using government programs, some of the destitute due to physical, mental capacity, or having suffered a devastating situation, can make "GoFundMe pages," and those not able to do that can find a helpful foundation. If determined and strong enough, they could start their own foundation, and for those who can't do either could access online sites with registered societal contributors for help. We've all seen people on the side of the road with a sign begging for money. Maybe they don't want to work or suffer from a serious mental illness. For these individuals, perhaps on-the-street social workers can be provided, sponsored by either public or non-profit sector entities. At the current time, we are not where we need to be as these methods can be difficult for many or hard to find and connect with.

There are continually new non-profit charity sites emerging and existing ones growing, such as: Doctors Without Borders; American Red Cross, The Nature Conservancy, Natural Resources Defense Council, St. Jude Children's Research Hospital, World Wildlife Fund, UNICEF USA, Save the Children, Disabled American Veterans Charitable Service Trust, and the American Society for the Prevention of Cruelty to Animals.

These are all a form of non-government redistribution of volunteered contributions. Without government departments, and if run ethically, they can be more efficient and effective to help the missing needs, but these and new ones need to be interconnected while keeping their autonomy by placing them into a global help network umbrella to which anyone can easily plug into a help source, and if unable, a family member or friend can do it for them. For example, if you were diagnosed with colon cancer, and your insurance will not cover the costs, you can look up and find the specific help group for your problem. Just like in a free market, missing help groups will emerge to fill in the holes.

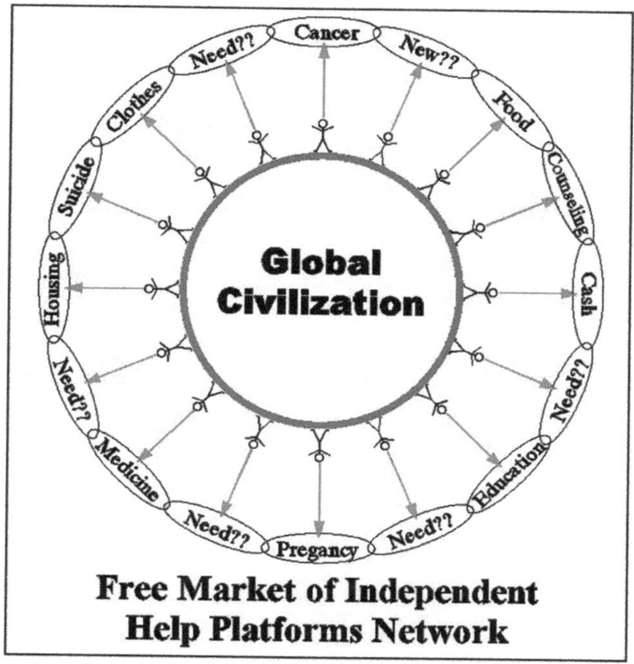

Free Market of Independent Help Platforms Network

According to the Nobel Prize-winning economist Milton Friedman, the government should not meddle with the free market through aid programs and minimum wages. In an interview he had with the economist John Phelan, on May 4, 2018, Milton said:

> *"The main way people have risen in the labor force is by getting unskilled jobs and learning things. Not merely technical skills: They learn such things as being at a job on time, spending eight hours a day at a job rather than standing around on street corners, having a certain element of responsibility, letting their employer know when they're not going to come in. All of those traits are very important. In an attempt to repair the damage that the minimum wage has done to traditional on-the-job training, you now have a whole collection of programs designed to take up the slack. The great proliferation of governmental programs in which employers are subsidized to provide on-the-job training gives employers an incentive to hire people*

> *and then fire them in order to get other people for whom they can get more subsidies."* Source: The American Experiment, Interview by John Phelan, |May 4, 2018]

In today's current state of affairs, the really ill and poor need to rely on government aid programs, but this "Band-Aid" approach is very top-heavy and inefficient. Milton Friedman had the idea of negative income tax, or NIT. It would help the poor and shrink government structure and wasteful spending with the money going directly to those less fortunate.

> *The NIT would replace all income programs with a simple cash payment to every citizen. If, for example, the payment were $6,000, a family of four with no income would receive an annual payment from the IRS of $24,000. For each dollar earned by members of that family, the payment would be reduced by some fraction—Friedman suggested possibly 50 percent. Thus, if the family of four receiving $24,000 earned $12,000 in a year, their net payment from the IRS would be $18,000 (the original $24,000 minus $6,000 tax on their earnings). But they would still have the $12,000 so their total income would increase to $30,000.*

> *Friedman's NIT is far better than most standard welfare programs for several reasons. First, working always pays more than not working. By contrast, many welfare programs do just the opposite—if you earn an extra dollar you lose two dollars of benefits. Second, instead of life for welfare recipients being "one endless visit to the Welfare Office," as author P. J. O'Rourke puts it, welfare recipients are freed to make their lives better. The NIT's cash payments replace the army of bureaucrats doling out food stamps, temporary assistance to needy families, Medicaid, Medicare, housing assistance, school breakfast and lunch, food stamps, rent subsidies, and the*

myriads of others. Source: Randy Simmons, *If You Really Want to Help the Poor, Remember Milton Friedman,* October 1, 2008

"About 1 in 5 Americans has some kind of disability, and 1 in 10 have a severe disability. Not only does this statistic affect those who are disabled, but individuals with disabilities not only endure disadvantages but so do their children or possibly grandchildren as they can potentially be left facing health care disadvantages as well as education." Source: US Census Bureau brief, report number 97-5.

More efficient grassroots efforts to help others less fortunate can replace existing government aid programs, but to do this, we first need to be strong ourselves. In the airlines, they teach us to put on our own mask first before helping others. A Desert Storm veteran who served as a medic while on tour, personally told me, "If you're hurt or not safe, you can't help anyone." ADDED TO ABOVE: PERSONALLY TOLD ME Over taxation can greatly reduce the helping ability of many, leaving more of the helping to government reliance.

As mentioned, a free market needs successful business owners to extend help to their employees and their families, being conscious of their business culture's impact, and again the super-rich needs to participate in their society, creating foundations and other charitable mechanisms for those less fortunate.

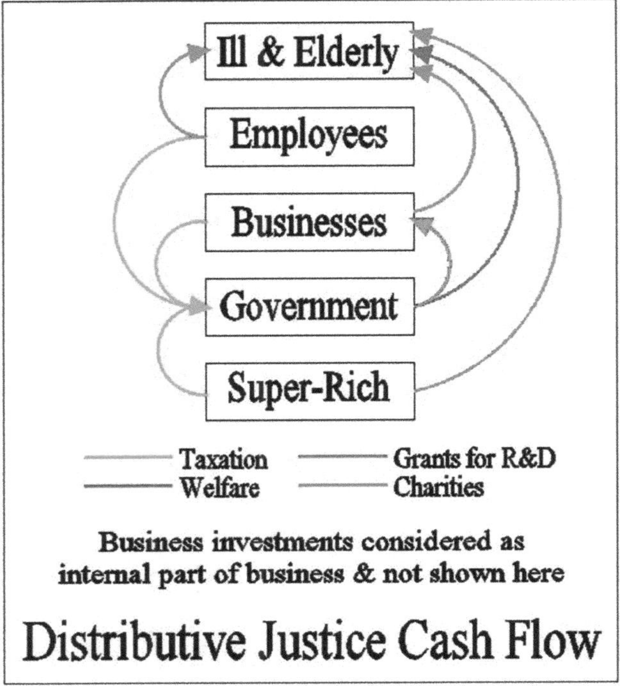

This is a form of distributive justice, where the excesses of those who fare well come to the aid of those who fare ill, and a process which requires little government involvement. Read more from *Distributive Justice, in the Internet Encyclopedia of Philosophy*. Source: https://iep.utm.edu/distributive-justice/

Societies with happy families are more content, creative, and contribute more to the greater whole than those where families are restricted, exploited, or unappreciated.

18b). Capitalism and the Management of the Planet and Universe – Our Basic Resource:

> *"The Earth will not continue to offer its harvest, except with faithful stewardship. We cannot say we love the land and then take steps to destroy it for use by future generations."* —John Paul II

This is also called “natural capital,” the primary base for our economy and existence.

This arm of capitalism requires exploration of the natural resources available and how best to use them for the long term. That would include ensuring their best continued viability . . . protecting the environment so that all of society and the future can be the beneficiaries.

Every village, city, and nation needs to create a natural mapping strategy, indicating where the most essential natural capital lies along with their related sensitivities and then incorporate it all into an intelligent, natural resource development and management plan. This could further be made into a “Natural Planetary Map,” indicating locations of the essential resources, a step toward global sharing, ethical harvesting, preservation, trade, and global sustainability, a limitless substrate to build from, and a bountiful pallet for any entrepreneur, bounded by only imagination that will inevitably lead to new resources and the mapping of extraterrestrial resources.

Of course, this sounds great, but what is to be done with the individuals who personally choose to cross the line from capitalism toward the hedonistic gratification of control, power, and greed?

Perhaps register them personally as ethical offenders as we do with pedophiles and other gross offenders.

Some markers identifying the actions of these miscreants include:

- Does it harm the environment?
- Does it cross moral/ethical boundaries?
- Does it make society/humanity better?

Today, the first marker listed needs some time to adjust, as many of our industries are currently trapped in environmentally harmful technologies through inheritance. The most obvious is our dependency on fossil fuels. A free first invisible hand always gives opportunity to creative private sector entrepreneurs, who will find healthier solutions from their passions and not from impositions. This freedom-based approach is always more effective than the government trying to expand itself with new departments to deal with these types of problems. Models for how this can work are explored in later Chapters.

A better government role could be for new businesses to fill out a survey with specific environment questions to determining whether their product or industry is helping, sustaining, or harming the environment, and if harming, a protocol must be submitted for review, amendments made and acceptance being required as applicable. Once up and running, any entity working with dangerous goods, materials, or in sensitive places must keep accurate records indicating safe storage, handling, mitigations, recycling, and disposal. Again, people need to be held severely personally accountable for any mishaps or cover-ups. Government departments must follow a similar process overseen by the Department of Environmental Protection and also held severely personally responsible and not allowed to hide inside a corporation or government shell.

It can't be overstated, the crux of our economic problem is always the individuals who choose to make terrible decisions. Governments and corporations are not evil, just like a car in a fatal accident is not charged with murder; governments and corporations are tools intended to improve society. If that person has evil tendencies, whether being your friend, running a corporation, government, or church under any ism, they will behave badly and need to be called out; it only takes one person to do so much damage.

19

Stock Market

Stock prices change every day by market forces. By this we mean that share prices change because of supply and demand. If more people want to buy a stock (demand) than sell it (supply), then the price moves up. Conversely, if more people wanted to sell a stock than buy it, there would be greater supply than demand, and the price would fall . . . Understanding supply and demand is easy. What is difficult to comprehend is what makes people like a particular stock and dislike another stock. This comes down to figuring out what news is positive for a company and what news is negative.
Source; Desjardins Online Brokerage, Feb., 01, 2021

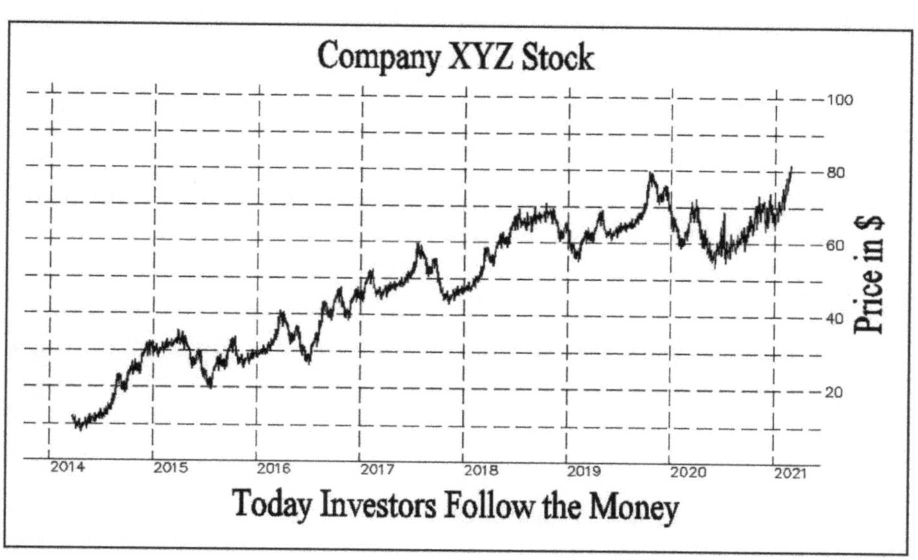

"The important things to grasp are the following:

1. *At the most fundamental level, supply and demand in the market determine stock price.*
2. *Price times the number of shares outstanding (market capitalization) is the value of a company. Comparing just the share price of two companies is meaningless.*
3. *Theoretically earnings are what affect investors' valuation of a company, but there are other indicators that investors use to predict stock price. Remember, it is investors' sentiments, attitudes, and expectations that ultimately affect stock prices.*
4. *There are many theories that try to explain the way stock prices move the way they do. Unfortunately, there is no one theory that can explain everything.*

> *"Public companies are required to report their earnings four times a year (once each quarter). Wall Street watches with rabid attention at these times, which are referred to as earnings seasons. The reason behind this is that analysts base their future value of a company on their earnings projection. If a company's results surprise (are better than expected), the price jumps up. If a company's results disappoint (are worse than expected), then the price will fall."* Source: Desjardins Online Brokerage, Feb., 01, 2021

As previously discussed, the stock prices today are controlled by the old adage of supply, demand, earnings, and rumors. Yes a bad incident on the news will drop the stock price, but the secret day-to-day goings on is not on the news, so stock prices soar, and daily bad behavior continues.

Where is the real picture of full disclosure? The stock market today has little concern for hidden unethical behavior. Full disclosure about a company's behavior with people and planet needs to be added.

20

Financial Market Reform

Current economic experts have many ideas regarding reform with few addressing the real problems. For example,

On CNBC News The former chief economist of the World Bank, Joseph Stiglitz, speaking on the covid crisis and the U.S. economy, said:

> *"It's time to rewire the U.S. economy: We shouldn't let a good crisis go to waste. You can get a two-for-one," he told CNBC's Steve Sedgwick at the annual Ambrosetti Forum on the shores of Lake Como in Italy. "The U.S. should, for example, invest in building 'green' infrastructure that creates jobs and helps bring down inequality, Stiglitz said. "Once you put your mind to it, you realize that we can attack two or three of these problems simultaneously," the 78-year-old said, adding that the U.S. has the labor and the capital. Stiglitz said it would be "healthy" for the U.S. economy to raise taxes "a little bit" to finance "some of the things we need for the common good."* Source; Sam Shead, CNBC, Economy: '*We shouldn't let a good crisis go to waste*', Sept. 3, 2021, 10:08 am EDT.

By raising tax rates to build new or larger government programs/departments with increased regulation as we've seen on the Control vs. Freedom chart, it will reduce sustainability. To change legislature to encourage and nurture private sector innovations does not require a tax increase and, in the 'real' picture it's successful entrepreneurs that bring in more growth and tax revenues. Real reform lays in freedom and morality, not government regulation and tax hikes.

> *"Free-market capitalism is the ethical highroad to human dignity and mutual prosperity. If its moral and related foundations can be successfully articulated to students in a persuasive manner, the totalitarian progressives can be met and opposed through the power of reason and a basic understanding of the connections between economic liberty, social peace, and mutual well-being for a better future for all of mankind."* By Richard Ebeling, a distinguished Professor of Ethics and Free Enterprise Leadership at The Citadel in Charleston, South Carolina. April 20, 2017

If someone offers you huge profits for doing little, would you take it even if you know people or our planet would suffer from this endeavor? This is the very question many of our world and industrial leaders have to deal with regularly, and sadly, many take the profits. It's a very tough situation to be in, but turning a blind eye and accepting this as normal, all in a day's business for profit, is simply greed with leanings of criminality.

> *"The more people rationalize cheating, the more it becomes a culture of dishonesty. And that can become a vicious, downward cycle. Because suddenly, if everyone else is cheating, you feel a need to cheat, too."* Quote by Stephen R. Convey.

This is exactly what happens every day around the world. Stocks from all economic isms: capitalist, socialist, and communist countries and some with gross human and environmental crimes all enter the trading floor as monetary equals, with little to no consequences for how they obtained their earnings.

New indicators representing the real impact on people and planet need to be put in place. Stock and world markets need to do more than just following the money. We need to know what the real impact is. Are these businesses helping or taking from our world? We need to be properly informed when we purchase their stock or products and what that purchase really encompasses.

Today, the most important question with any purchase is usually price first and quality second; however, there are so many more. Market disclosure is to ensure a fair price and authenticity of what you are purchasing. Some examples of non-disclosure would include you buying some art work, believing it to be an original, but nowhere is it identified as a copy, or you buy a used car that was repaired after a major accident without its disclosure. Each time, the seller gets paid more than what the item is worth because of secrets, but it's not equal for equal. The sellers feel they have done well for themselves, but in reality, it undermines the way business is supposed to work. It's a form of theft, creating a small economic imbalance. Every minute of every day, these types of transactions are taking place.

Can the same be said about the larger world-level transactions? When purchasing foreign-made products or stocks, we usually don't think about having a full market disclosure. The following questions need to be added:

1. Were the people who made it treated fairly?
2. What was the environment impact?
3. Is it sustainable?
4. Is it recyclable?
5. Did the country where it was made follow humane and environment protection programs?
6. Do we really need the item or product?
7. If consumable, is it healthy for us?

These all have a cost, locally, nationally, and in our global market. For example, Mom or Dad gets sick and die young because of their employ, or children working in abusive conditions; the water, soil, and air around the industry are toxified, affecting the surrounding population. Many of these shortcuts are never disclosed with attempts to even hide them, like the sleazy salesman example but on a much larger scale. Other countries simply dump their waste and toxics directly into the oceans, air, or ground, affecting the whole world.

One of these examples was with the gypsum board shortage in Florida as a result of a construction boom and the damages caused by the many hurricanes from 2004 to 2006, so Florida suppliers turned to China for the gypsum board. As a result, thousands of homes and offices spaces were contaminated with toxic fumes containing uranium, cadmium, beryllium, cobalt, lead, mercury, and other trace heavy metals. Many people lost their homes and savings to foreclosure, and many others got ill (my wife almost died). The air in your office or home was so harsh that it would change anything with copper or silver-black. This is an indication that China is not following safety measures when disposing these toxic chemicals as they simply ended up in the water table flow and nested in their calcium beds.

On the financial floors of the world, two major questions need to come about:

1. How do these companies with little regard for the seven questions listed above have their stock values on the same floor as other companies that pay money to follow civilized laws and ethics?

2. Who pays for all this? The companies that cut corners here are not on the same level playing field. In fact they are cheaters, cheating everyone. With an added monetary reduction for justice, equal for equal, these companies will quickly improve their destructive ways.

Another tactic used by the industry to get your money has to do with items 6 and 7 above, where advertising and educational propaganda create false narratives to make you believe their product is not just desirable but essential for your health.

For example, look at the dairy industry. Alissa Hamilton said:

> *We've had school milk programs and milk in schools since the beginning of the century. During World War II, we needed to boost milk production in order to make processed dairy products to send to soldiers overseas. But farmers weren't producing enough to meet this demand because they weren't getting paid enough. So the government decided, "Great, we'll create demand for milk by giving milk to our kids, and that way we'll have a demand for the fluid milk and we can make the processed products we need for soldiers . . . It's not all that surprising, because that's all we've heard. We've only heard from the dairy industry and government agencies that are built to support agricultural commodities like dairy. So you have the USDA creating the dietary guidelines — but it's also there to support agriculture. There's a conflict there.* Source; By Julia Belluz, *How we got duped into believing milk is necessary for healthy bones,* Apr 19, 2015

> *"The countries with the highest rates of osteoporosis are the ones where people drink the most milk and have the most calcium in their diets. The connection between calcium consumption and bone health is actually very weak, and the connection between dairy consumption and bone health is almost non-existent."* Source; By Amy Lanou Ph.D., Nutrition director for the Physicians Committee for Responsible Medicine, WA, D.C.

In reality, all we have to do is eat green leafy vegetables for calcium and bone strength, just like the cattle do.

Through proper disclosure, we, as consumers can know if we are supporting the greedy and reckless who fit better on the economic parasite side rather than on the symbiotic side. (See the Interaction Chart on page 21.)

The same can be said for governments that follow destructive patterns. Governments, like corporations, must behave and make decisions as an individual does and be held personally accountable if they don't. The current hiding behind a bureaucracy or industry must be eliminated through transparency and disclosure. Today, it's identifying the specific individual(s) in all nations and corporations worldwide making the good or bad choices and to receive their reward or punishment for justice due. It's ultimately always the population and planet who pay for the damage resulting from bad choices.

> *"Psychopathic behavior in the general population is about one in a 100. What's a little disturbing in this study is that not only are 21 percent of corporate executives psychopathic, but so is the same percentage of prison inmates."* Source: Washington Times, by Gene Marks, September 16, 2016.

This can most likely be said of many government leaders as well. Perhaps it's the psychopath, as a self-server narcissist, lacking in empathy, desiring fast gain, and cutting corners with little concern for what happens after they are gone.

According to an article written by Sara Lindberg on January 9, 2019 extracted from https://www.healthline.com/health/psychopath common signs of psychopathy include:

- *Socially irresponsible behavior;*
- *Disregarding or violating the rights of others;*
- *Inability to distinguish between right and wrong;*

- *Difficulty with showing remorse or empathy;*
- *Tendency to lie often;*
- *Manipulating and hurting others;*
- *Recurring problems with the law; and*
- *General disregard toward safety and responsibility.*

With ethical economic disclosure, societal shame may not hurt this type of character, but hurting them in what they care the most about, power and money, will. With ethical disclosure, many people will not support the companies doing bad things, domestically or internationally. Let each nation and the world know and be informed.

Without this disclosure, it's the lamb buying from the wolf selling. Anyone who knowingly supports endeavors that harm people or our planet is, in reality, supporting evil and, if on a larger scale, are partners to evil. By disclosing good and bad choices, a corporate culture is modeled, which must affect their stock demand and ultimately their prices.

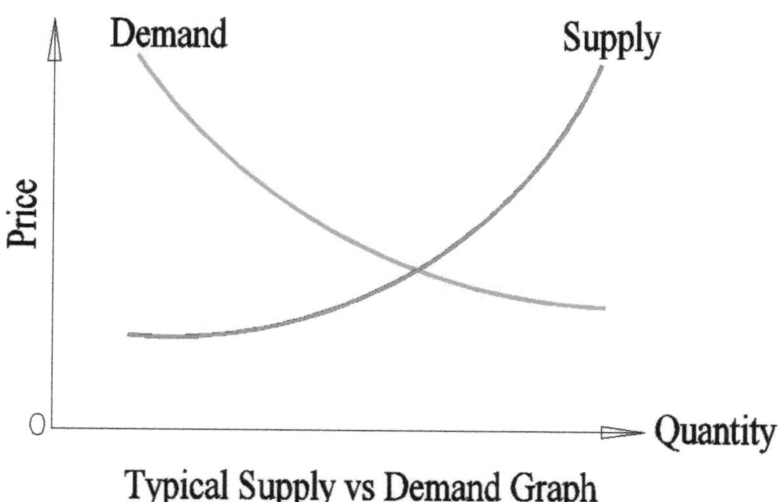

Typical Supply vs Demand Graph

Profit-motivated companies always place earnings first, and as history has shown, easily morph into unethical behavior with shareholder primacy being an example.

> *"The doctrine of shareholder's primacy is criticized for being at odds with corporate social responsibility and other legal obligations because it focuses solely on maximizing shareholder profits."* Source: *The truth about shareholder primacy*, by Gordon Pearson, 25 May 2012.

This rewards greedy selfish behavior with little regard for employees or the environment. The proper way needs to be reversed with the shareholder the least important as follows:

1. Planet 1st;
2. Customer 2nd;
3. Employee 3rd; and
4. Shareholder last.

It is only logical to put what you economically depend on first, being your resources, and then the outcome/results last. With this approach, our motivation becomes more connected to reality and the logic of what you depend on rather than chasing profits. This is much less destructive because it re-programs the subconscious to reduce short-cuts for a profit motive.

John Elkington, a British environmentalist and author, coined the term the "triple bottom line" in 1994, where he recognized the profit-loss bottom line was not an adequate measure of industries' real impact on the social-environmental situation, stating that, one, people, and, two, planet need to be accounted for as well. His idea was a great start to awaken capitalism's intended spirit, but the people part in the free-market industry is not one factor but rather two. Very importantly, one part is for the employees/workplace as a resource, and the other part is the benefactors (the global population). Source: *25 Years Ago I Coined the Phrase "Triple Bottom Line." Here's Why It's Time to Rethink It,* by John Elkington, June 25, 2018

For full disclosure and economic justice, real market value factors, besides industries' profit-loss statements, every company needs to complete a detailed report to identify three more key factors besides profit-loss for a "quadruple bottom line":

- Employee treatment and work place conditions;
- Environmental impacts; and
- Social contributions and corporate ethics.

Each of these can be further broken down as follows:

1. Employee treatment and work place: Includes a safe work place, fair wages for a respectful livelihood, educational/advancement opportunity, bonuses, profit sharing, and paid vacation time.
2. Environmental impact: To include safe cleanup and toxic wastes disposal, minimal pollution of any kind, increased recycling/biodegradability, sustainability of resources, and energy efficiency.
3. Social contributions and corporate ethics: Includes striving for constant improvements in 1 and 2 above, societal contributions, charities, public education, and so on.

So how can we know what companies and nations are really doing to their people and environment? We have many new abilities that did not exist during the time of our free-market founding fathers, and we now have the means to make some adjustments.

Perhaps using a five-star rating system added to the stock market based on these additional indicators, giving better disclosure of what investors are investing in.

By completing, say, quarterly reports as they do with earning, the indicators would show some measure of improvement or decline based on their choices, right along with their stock values over time. Reports would have to be collaborated by third-party means, including vlogs.

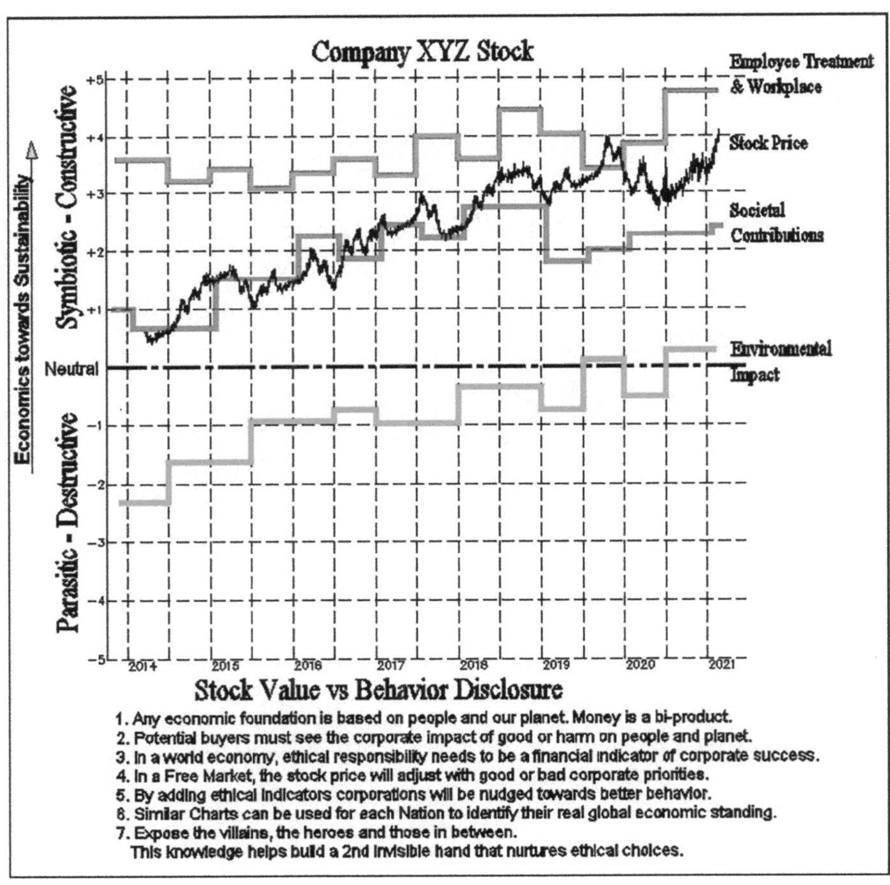

As consumers, this increased disclosure will build reputations available for all to see before investing or purchasing from them directly, thereby impacting their stocks on a traditional supply/demand chart like this:

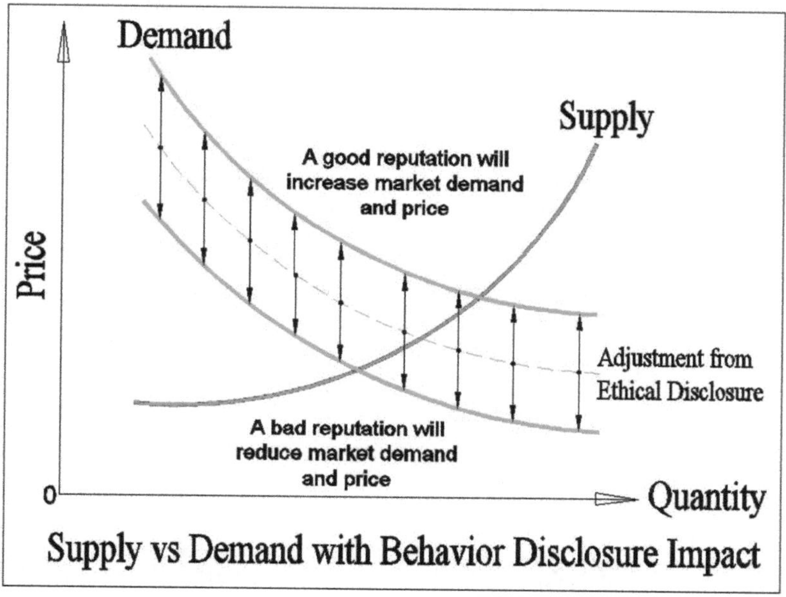

Supply vs Demand with Behavior Disclosure Impact

"Aristotle emphasized that virtue is practical, and that the purpose of ethics is to become good, not merely to know. Aristotle also claims that the right course of action depends upon the details of a particular situation, rather than being generated merely by applying a law." Source: Wikipediaen.wikipedia.org › wiki › *Aristotelian ethics* Extracted May 15, 2021

21

The Farmer's Principle

"The earth is not ours; it is a treasure we hold in trust for future generations." —A Namibian proverb

The farmer's principle is similar to "you reap what you sow," a metaphor about a trust based on choosing to sacrifice our best for others to benefit, and then almost magically, amazing things come back to us, and the cycle continues or even expands.

To continue this metaphor, each year, the successful farmer takes their best corn, pea, or whatever seeds, and instead of eating them, sacrifices these seeds to the soil, trusting for the best yield of crops.

Like the real capitalist who, through their abilities, seed with their best endeavor, then harvests the economic rewards, and lastly, shares their harvest for the community's benefit.

The farmer's soil and his best seed is the same as your risk balanced with the trust in your idea or ability. Both build something wonderful if done with ethics. It's amazing how simple things work when we have trust in the soil or our given abilities. Again, it's a much-needed cultural shift, putting the resources first and the results or expectations last.

The spirit of any endeavor always comes down to what motivates you to act. If it's greed, the end product will be compromised. When building something new, many choices need to be made, many with little thought, and many more subconsciously aligned with our deep-set motives. Greed always leads to fast short-term gains with less regard toward preserving the economic resources, natural or human.

If the motive is to be of service first and the results second, your choices will be to ensure your service is its best while protecting your needed resources through a cooperative relationship along the way. In a nutshell, if profit is your motive, then your real occupation is a profiteer, not a cabinet maker, and so on, but if your first motive is to build cabinets as your societal contribution, then you are a cabinet maker, and the money follows after. It's a simple mindset choice but one that can save business owners for falling into the abyss of shoddy products or services.

When one takes pride in one's talents and seeks to use them purely for selfish gain, it is a step toward being sociopathic. You, with talent, ability, drive, and energy, you are the ones responsible for planting the good seeds and giving back. We need to remember that what we were naturally given was not from our choice but rather by birth, fate, or God, whether from nature or nurture. Having an excess of ability, energy, opportunity, money, or any other resource, including one's virtue, carries a responsibly to share, which the life of any good civilization depends upon . . . a big part of the eudaimonic condition.

22

Ethical Treatment toward Service

"The best way to find yourself is to lose yourself in the service of others." Mahatma Gandhi, Source: https://www.greenwood-college.org/news-detail?pk=1102265

"Real success requires respect for and faithfulness to the highest human values-honesty, integrity, self-discipline, dignity, compassion, humility, courage, personal responsibility, courtesy, and human service." Quote by Michael E. DeBakey, surgeon and educator, Source: https://www.azquotes.com/quote/962700

When we find ourselves in any situation, good or bad, remember, everyone feels very much the same way. It's the basis of empathy and a much-needed reminder to be kinder, more patient, and helpful to uplift all those we come in contact with. This costs no money, some kind words, even a smile, and you've made the world a better place; it's that simple. We just have to remember to practice it regularly so that it becomes ingrained in who and what we are as individuals.

An important question related to our human relationships is, "What is the most valuable thing anyone has?"

It's time; the rich can't buy it. When someone does things for us, paid or not, we should call it "life-time," as each of us only has a finite amount of it. Economically and logically, this puts human service above all else, as service is time-giving. This important recognition is essential to healthy cooperation and a basis for eudaimonia in economics.

Oxford Languages defines service as, *"To repair, maintain or provide something to someone. ... Service is defined as someone or something that is intended to provide help to those providing assistance to others."* Source: https://www.oxfordlearnersdictionaries.com/definition/american_english/service

The super-rich must remember the condition of their privilege they find themselves, and when dealing with those providing service, they need to remember they are taking the workers' life-time away. In the big picture, service is more than one person doing something; it's them surrendering their finite time to assist another. The one being assisted usually sees this simply as a money payment for service and forgets the reality of this human interaction. We need to make an adjustment in our attitude, recognizing the human part of service, and give it more respect and thanks. When the rich treat working people as beneath them, it leads to disloyalty and unhappiness with the workers, the beginning of an unstable state of relationship, one history remembers with the rich being overthrown via disgruntled worker revolutions.

A similar cultural attitude can be found on how we see the blue collar as less than their white collar workers. It's a form of discrimination, as anyone trying to contribute to our economy and take care of their family needs to be respected. Humility is a cousin to empathy, so even if a person lacks the latter, perhaps some humility can give them a window to understand empathy.

When humility and empathy become embedded in our economic culture, we will place our interactions with people and the physical universe first above all things. A humble entrepreneur will always do better than the arrogant with the same skills because of openness to learn and being more user-friendly in human interactions.

> *"Without humility, you can't learn from others—and you certainly can't collaborate to solve problems."* Source; Tyndale, *The Power of Humility and Empathy*, April 22, 2019

By exercising these essential principles with those we hire, serve us, or are less fortunate than us, the concept of exploitation is minimized. Both sides of this equation will benefit with improved social stability and happiness. It's not about perfection, as that's impossible, but rather degrees of better cultural attitudes and healthy placement of priorities, all backed up with a corporate culture-policy and legislator that can nurture/encourage this good behavior.

Our growing social media and virtual posts can be used to improve employer-employee relationships, where prospective employees can view potential employers' cultures, being better informed of whom they want to work for based on good public or corporate behavior. This would also motivate employers to behave better.

In the near future, most of these service jobs will be replaced by machinery. There will be a shift in human contributions with new efforts to reinvent lost service-worker positions required in this new economy. There are many unknowns in how this shift will take place and how all these displaced people can contribute to care for themselves and their families. It will require new thinking and much effort, if not struggle for the world's transitioning. The good side of this is the mundane jobs will be done by machines, and we will all have more time to cooperate and be creative toward new opportunities, no matter what our personal capacity may be.

With this service-worker readjustment from robotic job displacement, is it very likely that in a matter of time technology will be free-thinking and smarter than us? This time frame is the critical path, perhaps more critical than any other. By practicing our humility toward all those who serve our daily lives now, we will be prepared for what is coming.

This raised humility and empathic attitude will lead to three new paths:

1. Put an end to social unrest and revolution from the working people;
2. It will save our planet through better environmental husbandry; and
3. It will teach our technology to not destroy us.

Point number 3 above may sound extreme, but if we don't change, we will simply pass this self-serving attitude on to the next revolution, human or not.

This threat was recognized by Makoto Nishimura (1883–1956), who designed and built a robot to exemplify good virtue. *"Concerned about the idea of robots seen as slaves to humans, particularly as portrayed in the play R.U.R., written by Karel Čapek, Nishimura set out to build a different kind of robot, or as he called it, an 'artificial human.' The robot he wanted to build would celebrate nature and humanity, and rather than a slave, it would be a friend, and even an inspirational model, to people."* Source, Frumer, Yulia (21 May 2020). "The Short, Strange Life of the First Friendly Robot". IEEE Spectrum. Retrieved 2020-06-30.

Most likely robots will surpass us in strength and knowledge and reach a point where they can reprogram themselves, rendering Isaac Asimov's three rules below useless:

> *"First Law: A robot may not injure a human being or, through inaction, allow a human being to come to harm.*
>
> *Second Law: A robot must obey the orders given it by human beings except where such orders would conflict with the First Law.*
>
> *Third Law: A robot must protect its own existence as long as such protection does not conflict with the First or Second Law."*

Source: Wikipedia, extracted July 27, 2021

In the not too distant future and with our current attitude toward service, this revolution could look like the artificial intelligence takeover movies we've all seen. We need to learn from Makoto Nishimura's friendly robot, to be kinder, emphatic, and grateful to improve our service culture now, as that servant will soon be a robot or maybe our assassin. By improving our moral example to those who serve us now, self-aware artificial intelligence can learn morals and virtues just as children do from good parents.

The renowned English theoretical physicist, cosmologist, and author Stephen Hawking (1942–2018) said,

> "*I fear that AI* (Artificial Intelligence) *may replace humans altogether. If people design computer viruses, someone will design AI that improves and replicates itself. This will be a new form of life that outperforms humans."*

To help this transition along, we need to recognize our current economic culture is upside down. The rich and big corporations need to be at the bottom, not on top. As mentioned, the very top must be our most vulnerable, our planet. It is the source of everything, then the ill/poor, followed by the people who work and provide services along with their families, then their bosses, then the corporations that own the stocks, and the rich at the very bottom.

It's like an upside-down pyramid of sorts, where a small, efficient, transparent government is simply the toothpick through the middle, from the top to bottom, holding it all together, kind of like a hero sandwich.

The government is a necessity, but it must stay in its place to maximize fair interaction and cooperation. This "toothpick," of course, must have temporary horizontal limbs to reach out in any layer but only for adjusting those when they choose to play unfairly. Just like in sports, the worst games are always those where the officials play too large of a role, affecting the victors rather than the talent of the players.

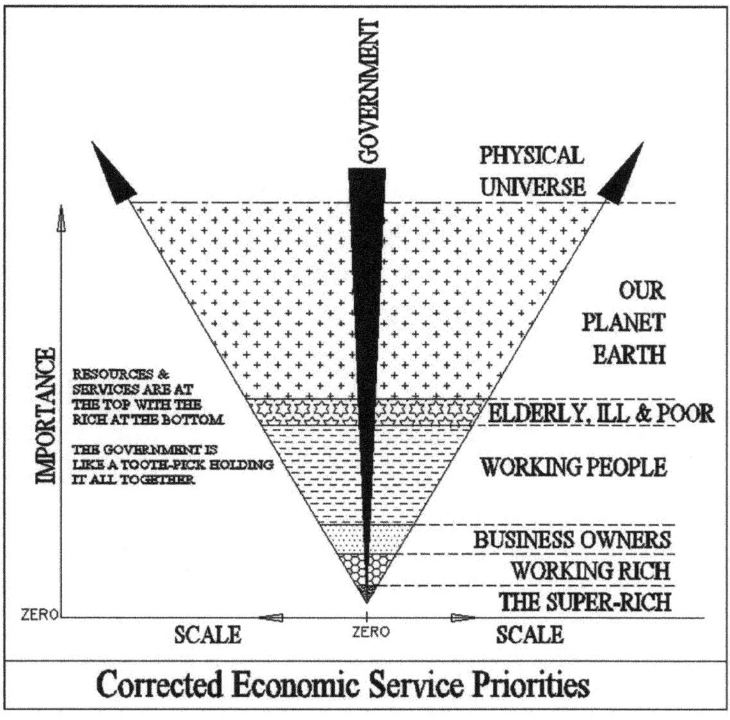

Corrected Economic Service Priorities

Logically, the highest priority needs to be given to the most vulnerable and dependent on our good behavior, being our earth, and the less fortunate.

Hero Sandwich

This diagram shows the opposite of our current cultural attitude, in which the rich are considered upper class and our earth and working people are there to be exploited. As one of the mantras in this book, the small number of individuals at the bottom of this diagram needs to join humanity by contributing their excess to everything above them. The government pierces and protects all economic realms and is small so as not to burden the working people with high taxation and not over regulate the entrepreneur. A small government can provide the needed infrastructure and basic core essentials, with ideals based on the highest social and environmental standards, maximizing freedoms and opportunity for all to voluntarily cooperate, yet swift to enforce punishment for greedy or power-lust individual behavior, just like our primitive cultures once did. As history is a testimony, bad choices, such as greed, corruption, and the gathering of riches without sharing can be found in all economic isms, whether public, private, or religious.

23

Countering Greed and Corruption

Corruption in the public sector is very common in developing nations, where corrupt government officials demand bribes from the working people when requiring their services. On all national levels, high-ranked officials and politicians often engage in secretive side deals for personal gain. And in the private sector, there are multitudes of ways to cheat, limited only by one's imagination.

Today, the need for improved ethics is greatly in want, with the accelerated growth we have experienced in our technologies since the mid 1800s to the present. Technology has become one of the main forces changing our social, economic, and political world. It has also reduced the value of labor through robotics and the virtual worlds of big-tech. This, along with the new discoveries in communications, medicine, transportation, pharmaceuticals, and so on, has led to the emergence of many more super-rich entities and individuals with some lacking in benevolence, behaving as demigods watching us, categorizing, forming, and selling marketing tools based on what we do, where we go, and what we like and think about. Others with so much wealth are no longer participating within our world's reality except to manipulate it to serve their personal interests.

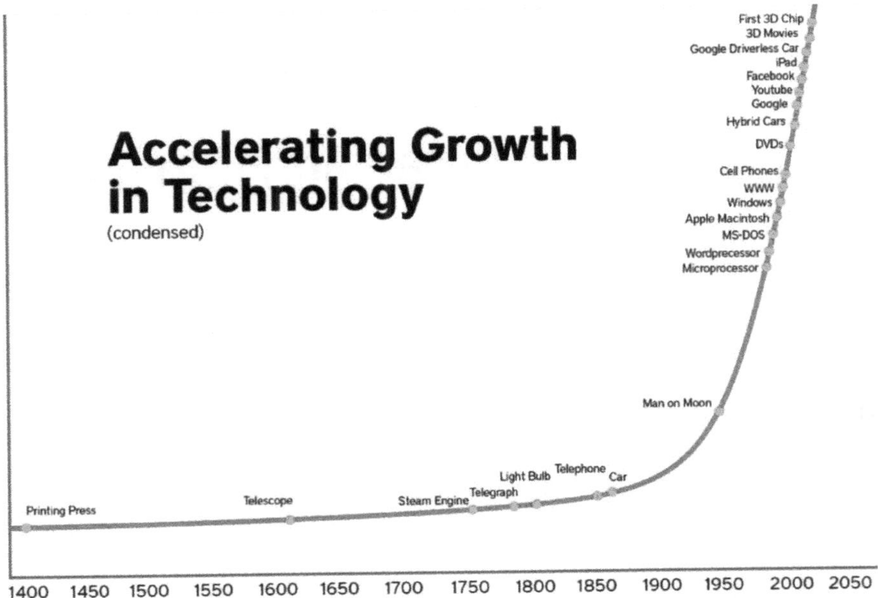

Source; PBRG, Legacy Research Group, August 18, 2020

> *"Money and markets have been around for thousands of years. Yet as central as currency has been to so many civilizations, people in societies as different as ancient Greece, imperial China, medieval Europe, and colonial America did not measure residents' well-being in terms of monetary earnings or economic output."*

> *"In the mid-19th century, the United States—and to a lesser extent other industrializing nations such as England and Germany—departed from this historical pattern. It was then that American businesspeople and policymakers started to measure progress in dollar amounts, tabulating social welfare based on people's capacity to generate income. This fundamental shift, in time, transformed the way Americans appraised not only investments and businesses but also their communities, their environment, and even themselves."* Source; The Atlantic, *How Money Became the Measure of Everything*, By Eli Cook, October 19, 2017

For stability, ethical growth must run in balance with technological growth; otherwise, the technologically advanced civilization will enter an unstable state, much like the explosive chemistry example previously mentioned.

> *"A good use of technology is one which improves human physical, mental, spiritual, and moral well-being. It helps people become healthier, more educated, more loving of God and neighbor, and better at making moral decisions. A bad technology will do the opposite: make us sicker, less educated, less loving of others, and worse at making moral decisions. Technology often simply makes actions easier–and we want good technology that will facilitate good actions, not bad technologies that will facilitate bad actions."* Source; Santa Clara University, *The Relationship of Morality and Technology*, by Brian Green, A. director of Campus Ethics.

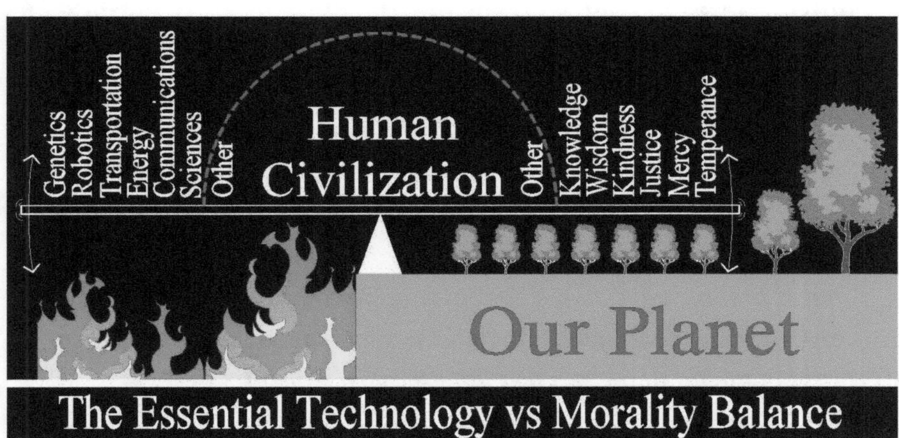

The Essential Technology vs Morality Balance

Technology versus morality imbalances require our ethical choices to be raised. Today, we see the technology-morality gap widening exponentially, one of its 'fruits' being the widening disparity of wealth. This morality gap needs to be reeled in from the ground up. The founding of the internet can help counter this with its natural side effect of increased transparency.

This relatively new and expanding trend is an opportunity, never available until the last few decades, yet even with this growing transparency, there are those who still try to hide in the shadows. The internet is organic in nature, in every corner of the planet, accessible, inexpensive, easy to wield, and with real social movement platforms that will increase public awareness toward a higher standard of expectation, where corruption can be pinpointed and exposed.

As of April 2022, there were five billion internet users worldwide, or 63 percent of the global population, opening up an organic grassroots opportunity to expose the parasites from the earnest. Source: https://www.statista.com/statistics/617136/digital-population-worldwide/

This social movement process through the internet has already begun in India, exposing the bad and acknowledging the good players:

> *In August 2010, a non-profit organization called Janaagraha launched a website www.ipaidabribe.com* (IPAB) *where people are encouraged to share their encounters with corrupt officials (and honest officials) anonymously. The website provides a snapshot of bribe occurrences in a city. It promises to "use them to argue for improving governance systems and procedures, tightening law enforcement and regulation and thereby reduce the scope for corruption in obtaining services from the government."*

> *"According to the website statistics (as of September 2014 – little over four years since the website was founded), there were 28,454 reports of bribery from 725 cities across the country amounting to Rs. 226.24 crores (US$ 37.7 million approx.), which shows the width and depth of petty corruption in India. The website also*

boasts of more than 4.5 million visitors, underscoring the interest of the Indian public in matters regarding corruption." Source; *Can social media and the internet reduce corruption?* By Chandan Jha, Assistant Professor of Finance, Oct. 21 2014

Because of India's success with the "I Paid A Bribe" (IPAB) site against government corruption, *"IPAB has been replicated, with various degrees of success, in over 26 countries all around the world, including Greece, Hungary and Serbia in Europe, Mexico and Colombia, in the Americas, Morocco, Kenya, Nigeria and Zimbabwe in Africa, and Pakistan, Philippines and Asia."* Source; U4 Expert Answer, *The potential of online corruption-reporting initiatives,* Extracted Aug. 23, 2021

These are all a tremendous start, and being fledging, there are some problems to be resolved. Here are some in brevity, based on U4 Expert Answer:

1. Being anonymous, it is difficult for a complaint be verified as real;
2. Being anonymous makes follow-up loops difficult, so many complaints end up more as statistics rather than justice being delivered, but it can draw attention to anomalies with government workers or their departments;
3. The rural or poor people do not have access to the internet or are not savvy enough to do so;
4. The reporting is more active with specific news breaks and reduces afterward. It needs more "steam" to stand on its own; and
5. With the diversity of cultural contexts, no one corruption reporting platform fits all.

There is a sixth not mentioned above; being IPAB only focuses on the public sector and not on what industry and commerce is doing. As shown in the Financial Market Reform section, the industry disclosure needs to include the level of cooperation in these three indicators:

1. Employee treatment and work place conditions;
2. Environmental impacts; and
3. Societal contributions.

There are existing organizations like: Transparency International, U4 Anti-Corruption Resource Centre, "As You Sow," CDP, Violation Tracker, The Better Business Bureau, and many more. But more still need to be built. Some could be purely environmental, others human rights and corruption, and others about societal contributions, all open online for anyone offer help, comment, provide evidence, or simply view.

These "out-into-the-sunlight" sites can create a sense of pride or shame, impacting sales, thereby pressuring sociopathic behavior to evolve a social conscious, and as mentioned, inform us where best to spend or invest.

Customers, employees, factory neighborhoods, and anyone affected by a business can enter good or bad information pertaining to how any business or government chooses to behave. The integrity of this process must be very serious and verifiable. Huge fines or other punishments must be made clear for false claims of good or bad. The details of this information process needs much development to ensure its validity to best protect and expose the real corporate situation in relation to the specific new ethical market indicators.

The world map below is a corruption perception index (CPI) and was created in 2020 by Transparency International, which began in Germany in 1993. The deeper color toward red, the more corrupt the country. These ratings are calculated based on thirteen different data sources and twelve different institutions that capture perceived corruption. Visit https://www.transparency.org/en for more information.

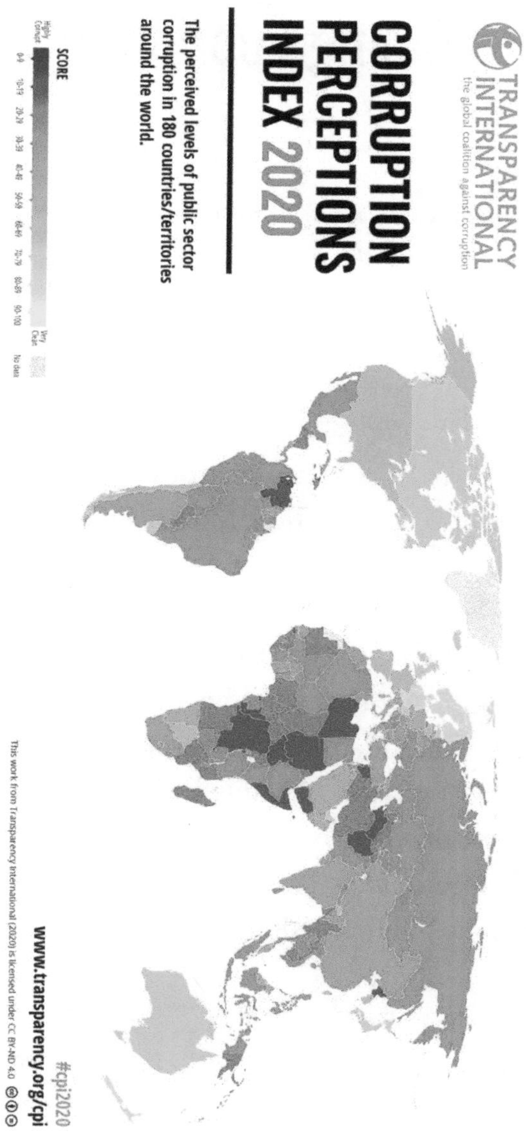

From this map, it is clear that our world is in serious trouble. There is still so much to be done to expose these cheaters.

24

Facing Economic Disparity

"The life of money-making is one undertaken under compulsion, and wealth is evidently not the good we are seeking; for it is merely useful and for the sake of something else." Quote by Aristotle in *Nicomachean Ethics.*

With lots of money, you don't have to connect or engage with people or things. You can just throw money at people and things with minimal real interaction. Most of us have had experiences with little money; for example, when I was fourteen, I wanted to go to the Canadian National Exhibition but could only scrounge ten dollars. With such limited funds, I had to engage with everyone and every opportunity, forced to connect with the real experiences. A few years later, I went with $150 and, by comparison, required much less interaction as I could just get what I wanted when I wanted it. Sadly but enlightening, it was nowhere near the original experience or fun. The super-rich have forgotten this. No one person needs to have hundreds of millions, let alone billions of dollars.

It is great for the individual who creates such wealth—congratulations, outstanding—but now it's time to give back in measures relative to your net worth. This is very important because what is given must be proportionate to what is still possessed. For example, if the average person gives $100, that is a lot of money, yet $100,000 for a super-rich person may relatively be pennies.

These individuals are not capitalists but just very greedy people. Going back to Adam Smith, the free market is the heart of capitalism and, as pointed out approximately 200 years ago, for it to work, it requires these personal choices:

1. Feel much for others and less for ourselves;
2. To restrain our selfishness;
3. To indulge our benevolent (well-meaning) affections;
4. To constitute the perfections of human nature; and
5. Produce a harmony of sediments and passions among humanity.

To reiterate, in any well-functioning system, those with knowledge or means have a given responsibility to share. These excesses need to be used actively in any societal development and not simply left to stagnate, locked in one's avaricious material accumulations and accomplishments.

Today, we see a few of these super-rich doing something for good, like Warren Buffet or Bill and Melinda Gates, but many use their money to remain out of the public eye, contributing nothing in the real economic picture unless it feeds their debauchery through money sway or the control of elected officials.

If we stopped sharing our love, time, and knowledge, we, as a species, would end, but why is it now acceptable not to share one's wealth? Are our given capacities in life not directly proportional to our responsibility to give back and share our excesses?

How did this "non-culture" of the super-rich begin and pretend to be acceptable? Perhaps it began when one person broke morality with their excessive hording and became super-rich. Then others thought if they can do it, so can they, and they, too, begin to emulate this narcissism. Then more and more joined, giving false justification for this inhuman behavior, making it acceptable amongst them like a club. The quote from the 1980s by Malcolm Forbes is the epitome of this, *"He who dies with the most toys, wins."* He may have said this tongue and cheek, but his comment reminded the world of this gross disparity, making serious cultural shock waves.

Joking or not, it's a mocking of all those with little hope for food, shelter, and basic necessities of life, let alone purchasing toys. It's a 100 percent complete disconnect and a very sad state of mentality, especially when only a few hundred of these super-rich have the means to solve most of the world's problems. See "1-pixel wealth" to follow.

Time always exposes the truth, so to you, with great excesses and not sharing, remember, time goes by very fast, and you, too, will soon be gone, so while you live, take this opportunity to feed your narcissism and leave a legacy for all the ages as someone who helped appease so much human suffering. It is a choice given to only a very few, as outlined below.

Your name can be remembered as that of a great philanthropist associated with a saga of many good doings to reduce poverty, disease, reduce population growth through education, and build great centers for higher learning, advancements in "green" technologies, and so on.

Or

Join the ranks to be remembered as the hedonist, greedy, villain, the psychopath, being fully aware of the current suffering and death you stood over and did nothing to help, while continuing to buy more, feeding your endless indulgences.

From an article in Forbes,

> *When it comes to financial wealth (which includes investable assets such as cash, equities, funds and bonds), the share controlled by HNWIs (High net worth individuals) is even larger at 40%. The amount of financial wealth in the world reached $250 trillion in 2020, having grown 8.3% despite the pandemic's worst effects. . . Forbes annual billionaires list now includes 2,755 billionaires, who collectively grew their wealth from $8 trillion in 2020 to $13.1 trillion this year. Boston Consulting Group predicts this wealth is only going to increase over the next five years, surpassing the half-quadrillion dollar mark as major economies claw back their pandemic losses.* Source: Ollie A Williams, Forbes Senior Contributor, Wealth Management Jun 10, 2021,12:00am EDT

According to *1-Pixel Wealth,* created by Matt Korostoff, just the top 400 richest Americans could solve so many American and world problems and still be billionaires. See the pie chart he created below. This money does not include other rich countries, such as China and Europe. This chart shows human suffering does not need to exist but is simply and sadly allowed to continue because of a few hundred people in the world who are choosing not to help.

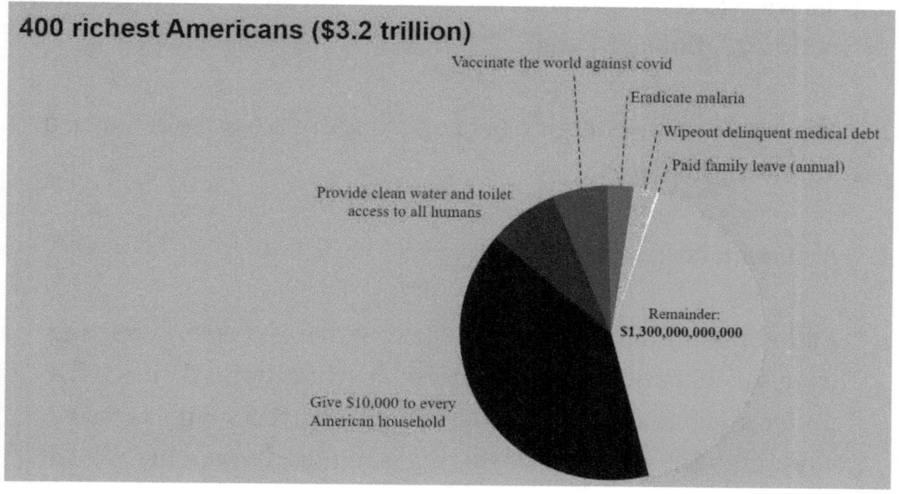

Source: https://mkorostoff.github.io/1-pixel-wealth/, Updated April 3rd, 2021

> *It is the moral obligation of the rich class to help the needy, poor and those who can't afford bread and butter even once during the day. Don't take it negatively!! But, if you will invest a certain percentage of your income in helping the poor, this will help purchase the contraceptive device, increase education opportunities thus helping in population control and more and more people becoming well educated. This can also decrease the rate of population growth thus saving the precious environmental resources from depletion.*
> Source: Get Do Help, *Why the rich should help the poor*. Extracted August 19, 2021.

The super-rich who refuse to give back in proportion to their excesses are the missing link for any ethical society. Many today use their power to pay little taxes and their voluntary giving is relatively little if at all. Through our personal choices within the free market, we can stop their cash flow simply by shutting them down at the source through boycotts, by supporting their more ethical competitors, or encouraging new smaller entities to replace them. For social media, some simple ways to re-divert billions of dollars toward good are identified in Section 25, Social Media.

For those who refuse to give back, perhaps more extreme measures are required, such as:

1. A financial cap:

   Rather than stifling the entrepreneur with high taxation starting from the inception of their venture, let them build their wealth under a fair tax structure, but when they reach an excessive amount, have a cap where sharing is required. But what would the amount be, and would it be government-mandated or voluntary? Say, you, as the CEO of a corporation, earns an annual net income over $50 million, and you and your firm gets registered to give your excesses toward societal contributions. To stick with the organic, let's make it voluntary; however, it would be public knowledge, whether you did or did not contribute. Maybe lawmakers give a different number than the $50 million cap, but overall, the number comes back to the economic condition of the day per province, state, nation, and the opinion of the peers. The voluntary approach is more transparent and efficient, with the aid going directly to whom or what needs it.

2. A net earning versus charitable contributions registry:

   A website that identifies those with annual earnings, including bonus, expense accounts, and so on, above, say $50 million, where their contributions toward helping are made public along with what the percentage it is of their net worth. Sadly, this would be a form of redistribution involving the government's justice system. However, it can be compared to us taking needed medicine when we are ill, where the government's intervention in this situation would be much like a societal laxative; it would certainly help move things along.

3. Make all social media sites charitable organizations with a cap of 5 percent administration fees. Explained in the social media chapter, with no more billions of dollars 'stolen' because we continue to essentially communicate as we've always done.

4. Make this non-sharing a criminal offence:

   In the free market theft, bribery, fraud, and extortion all break the law and are criminal, so why not add extreme narcissism clearly visible by hording wealth and not sharing? This would have to go hand in hand with a financial cap so not to be abused by those enforcing such a law.

> *The inordinate disparity between rich and poor, a source of acute suffering, keeps the world in a state of instability, virtually on the brink of war. Few societies have dealt effectively with this situation. The solution calls for the combined application of spiritual, moral and practical approaches. A fresh look at the problem is required, entailing consultation with experts from a wide spectrum of disciplines, devoid of economic and ideological polemics, and involving the people directly affected in the decisions that must urgently be made. It is an issue that is bound up not only with the necessity for eliminating extremes of wealth and poverty but also with those spiritual verities the understanding of which can produce a new universal attitude. Fostering such an attitude is itself a major part of the solution.* Source, The Universal House of Justice: The Promise of World Peace, pp. 10-11, Haifa, 1985

This disparity of wealth is an immoral human evolutionary trend that will pass, but for how long and with how much more suffering?

25

Social Media

The Top 10 Social Media Sites chart below shows a total of 10.491 billion participants. The monthly average users (MAU) are greater than the current world population, indicating that many people use multiple sites.

		MAU	Revenue	Launched	Headquarters
1	Facebook	2.7 billion	$86 billion	2004	Menlo Park, CA
2	YouTube	2 billion	$19.8 billion	2005	San Bruno, California
3	Whatsapp	2 billion	$5 billion	2009	Menlo Park, California
4	Instagram	1.16 billion	$6.8 billion	2010	Menlo Park, CA
5	TikTok	689 million	$35 billion	2016	Culver City, CA
6	Snapchat	433 million	$911 million	2011	Los Angeles, CA
7	Reddit	430 million	$212.5 million	2005	San Francisco, CA
8	Pinterest	416 million	$1,693 million	2010	San Francisco, CA
9	Twitter	353 million	$3.72 billion	2006	San Francisco, CA
10	LinkedIn	310 million	$8.05 billion	2003	Mountain View, CA

Top 10 Social Media Sites and Platforms 2020

Source; Search Engine Journal, by Shelley Walsh, *The Top 10 Social Media Sites & Platforms 2021*, June 22, 2021

These platforms have become an integral part to all our daily lives, a means to share and freely cooperate without issues of borders, travel, or time.

> *"Social media marketing is an effective way for you to connect with leads interested in your business, deliver tailored content, and build relationships that nurture followers towards conversion. This strategy is an excellent option for making a one-on-one connection with leads."* Source; WebFX, *Is Social Media Marketing Worth It? 6 Reasons to Use Social,* By Macy Storm, Aug. 29, 2020

The more "hits" these platform get, the more businesses want to place their ads for public viewing, and the more revenues the social media sites make.

> *"Today, we understand advertising is the lifeblood of all the big social networks. Paid social media has become a key component of many brands' marketing strategies. The more people these platforms have access to, the more money they make from businesses selling those people their products."* Source; *Why Social Media is 'Pay to Play' in 2021,* by Neil Patel, extracted Oct. 09 2021.

All the founders/owners of these social media sites have become new members to the super-rich.

> *"Advertising revenue, which continues to be the bulk of Facebook's income, rose 56 percent to $28.6 billion, easily surpassing Wall Street expectations. Roughly 3.51 billion people now use one of Facebook's apps every month, up 12 percent from a year earlier."* Source, The New York Times, by Mike Isaac, Jul 28, 2021.

Looking at these ad revenues, along with the over 10 billion participants, the cash flow is staggering; combined, they would be well over $100 billion per annum. To put this into proper perspective, we need to identify who is benefiting from all this money. Yes, families and businesses get to stay in touch and grow from their internal interactions, but they are kept outside of the big money. These relatively new "social" platforms are, in reality, Trojan horses, being more corporate from which just a few individuals take the "big" money.

Sharing with family, loved ones and businesses has always been a key part of social freedom, and the new technology of the internet has made it a lot easier, but it comes with some hidden costs. In reality, the creators of these social media platforms are tapping this essential interaction like a parasite, a tapeworm of sorts. As with all new technologies, we see the advantages of the new opportunity while something else is compromised. In this case, once a user, we enable big-tech to milk it, taking in multi-billion dollars to feed a few narcissists.

These essential social interactions, like breathing, have always been free, and today we've been caught off guard with our new toys integral with strings attached.

A societal adjustment is needed for better use of this new technology, one that removes the parasites while loved ones and businesses can continue to share on these or new sites.

The billions of dollars from these sites with a very simple adjustment can shift this money to those with real needs and thereby help level our global economic disparity. These interactions then become real social media rather than the super-rich corporate syphoning as we see today.

See the diagram below.

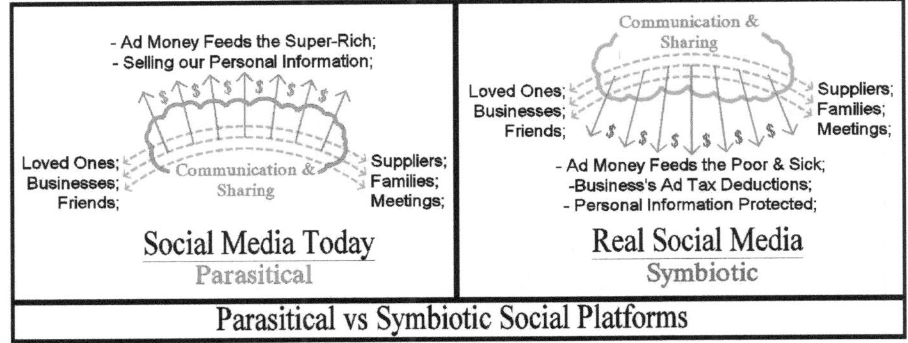

This restructuring can be greatly encouraged by:

1. Register the symbiotic type social media platform as a charity with the government;
2. Ensure the business ads placed on these charity type sites are tax deductible because the money goes to help communities, poor villages, and so on;
3. Build public awareness that these new social media sites help the needy and not the greedy;
4. Ensure users know how to use the social media sites to help the less fortunate;
5. Make it a criminal offense for these new non-profit social media sites to sell your personal information; and
6. Cap the non-profit administrative costs to fall within the maximum allowable charity administration charges of the gross revenues. These fees need to be clearly identified with public transparency.

These fees based on what the "charity.lovetoknow.com" site can be as follows:

- *Food pantries/banks and humanitarian supply charities should have lower overhead with a cap of costs around three percent.*

- *Grant-making organizations shouldn't see costs higher than seven and a half percent.*

Source, *Charities Administrative Expenses*, By Michele Meleen, extracted June 04, 2022.

How amazing when businesses help themselves by advertising, and their ad payments go toward the less fortunate. Everyone wins, and the super-rich get only a very small part of the billions under this very humane restructuring.

To put this into real dollars, let's take one of the current, smaller social medias with annual revenues at $5 billion dollars. The model proposed here is both a humanitarian supply and grant-maker type charity, making the administration fee 5 percent. $5,000,000,000 × 0.05 = $250,000,000. That is still a huge annual income, which as an example that can be further broken down as follows: CEO: $50 million annually, fifty tech engineers ("star talent") at $3 million each, and the remaining $50 million for offices, clerical, and so on costs, while $4.5 billion goes to help the world from just one small media charity site.

These restructured sites will be better favored by businesses because their ad payments now become charitable tax deductible donations to help the poor, while at the same time marketing their wares. This restructuring will cut into the few individuals getting the billions, a process very much like a *"Robin Hood effect,"* where the poor win by stopping the cash flow to the super-rich and change the course of profit-seeking businesses, where the owners may not even care, but, regardless, become donors to help the needy because they save taxes. This is a big step toward a eudaimonia-like free-market, where advertising businesses can make profits, and the people in need become the new social media shareholders/beneficiaries. The dots just have to be joined for so many to win without growing more government.

Given the choice, which social platforms would you use?

1. Sites that support the super-rich; or
2. Sites that help reduce wealth disparity and help the needy?

Of course these symbiotic non-profit platforms will have to grow enough to compete with the existing giants, but with the incentives listed above, it should not take long for the corporate parasite sites to be humbled to change or go out of business through the workings of the free market first invisible hand, allowing hundreds of billions of ad revenue dollars to go toward helping the growth of a second invisible hand.

If none of the existing owners will switch to a charity status, then the social media users must rise in protest or boycott for someone of means to become a true hero by stepping forward.

Once one platform switches or a new one starts as a charity, the impact on humanity would be much larger than the invention of the printing press. For example:

> *The printing press was the great innovation in early modern information technology, but economists have found no macroeconomic evidence of its impact. This article exploits city-level data. Between1500 and1600, European cities where printing presses were established in the 1400s grew 60% faster than otherwise similar cities. Cities that adopted printing in the 1400s had no prior advantage, and the association between adoption and subsequent growth was not due to printers choosing auspicious locations. These findings are supported by regressions that exploit distance from*

Mainz, Germany—the birthplace of printing—as an instrument for adoption. JEL Codes: N13, N33, N93, O11, O18, O33. Source, *Information Technology and Economic Change: the impact of the printing press,* by Jeremiah E. Dittmar, extracted by Federal Reserve Bank, 11 May 2020.

The global impact of these real, symbiotic social media sites would:

1. Share all vital human excesses, including billions of dollars, knowledge, and technology;
2. Reach a much larger population;
3. Be much more easily accessed;
4. Help the worst global conditions and situations immediately; and
5. Provide a long, overdue healing opportunity for the world.

26

A Second Invisible Hand—A Cultural Awakening

"Less known is the second invisible hand, which refers to individuals' sense of sympathy toward others. In Theory of Moral Sentiments, he (Adam Smith) acknowledges how human beings' sense of attachment and desire to help others can, likewise, influence their economic behavior." Source: The Manila Times, *A second 'invisible hand' – Is this what drives social entrepreneurs?* By Raymond Habaradas, February 27, 2018

Simply put, one invisible hand yields the excesses, and the second invisible hand helps share it, each driven by internal forces relevant to specific in-time-place circumstances without regulation.

"We are not rich by what we possess but by what we can do without." —Immanuel Kant

This statement from Kant clearly speaks of our excesses.

Through much increased world disclosure, a second hand will evolve, call it an awakening . . . an awareness that wakes you from the slumber of familiarity and comfort, connecting the current single invisible hand with the living global context of our morality.

With the growing World Wide Web and social media, we see the fledging emergence of this awakening through funding movements, such as Heartfelt Connector, a philanthropic organization that helps connect the rich, businesses, and nonprofits to help those less fortunate.

As these and new watchdog/help organizations continue to expand and overlap around the world, they will be subject to the workings of the first invisible hand, filling in help/protection opportunities, become more efficient and innovative within a free market of need, and growing empathy and sympathy. The definition of empathy and sympathy and how they differ is important for this second hand to blossom.

> *"Empathy means experiencing someone else's feelings. It comes from the German Einfühlung, or 'feeling into.' It requires an emotional component of really feeling what the other person is feeling. Sympathy, on the other hand, means understanding someone else's suffering. It's more cognitive in nature and keeps a certain distance."* Source: 6seconds the Emotional Intelligence Network, *Empathy vs. Sympathy: What's the Difference?* Extracted, January 16, 2022.

Nobel Economics Prize winner, Milton Friedman, said, *"We're here to try to make the world a little better than we found it."*

We see people everywhere we don't know. Some can appear weird in movement or have verbal or physical abnormalities. Every person on our planet is like the ocean's surface. In them, we see moments of calm and storm but only learn their reality when we take a risk to delve into their depths and discover their secret richness within . . . sometimes falling in love. Let's not forget most of the world is born into contextual disadvantages, such as poverty or dysfunctionality. This is not about government redistribution as history has shown its clandestine suffering. This is about accepting and igniting each of our inner emphatic abilities and reaching out. Without it, we're not experiencing and participating in being truly human.

If each of us could tune in at any time and hear the cries and see the images of pain, suffering and victories that go on all around us all over the world at any minute, it would probably render us dumbstruck. When we are uninformed, it is easy to pretend all is well, do nothing, and just carry on with our busy lives. But what if there was a way to bring each of us closer to the real conditions in the world? It would certainly be an awakening.

This awakening would have to be one with minimal regulation and oversight so it can operate hand in hand in full cooperation with the free market. It can awaken the desire for cooperation and sharing and recognize good behavior by providing due reward from a new social conscious, a form of cultural empathy, often not present in our individual political and corporate leaders. Through the development of the existing and the birth of new watchdog/help platforms, the bad can be found, shut down, and the good people honored.

Each troubled, struggling, or developing village, town, city, or country can create a virtual picture of what each sees a decent life needs to be. A virtual picture that includes the resources they see are required, each specific to their culture, geography, climate and so on. Through locally trained IT persons, each can custom build their own "flower" of sorts. It would include time accurate or live-streaming images of what the populace is coping with, affecting the children, the family unit, education, health care, housing, transportation, food, and water, and so on.

Once every place in need has made a "flower," they would be linked together, forming a garden of cultural diversity in real-time of our world's developmental needs, suffering, successes, and beauty. If the locally identified main problem is corruption, then that issue can connect with watchdog corruption organization's report platforms; if it's environmental, those appropriate watchdogs can help; facilities like health centers, schools, and so on can connect to appropriately help organizations, charities, or foundations with priorities, always from the local's perspective and not from outsiders. This will give the world a live entry to experience the real social, economic, and cultural situation of anywhere as long as they have a viewing platform.

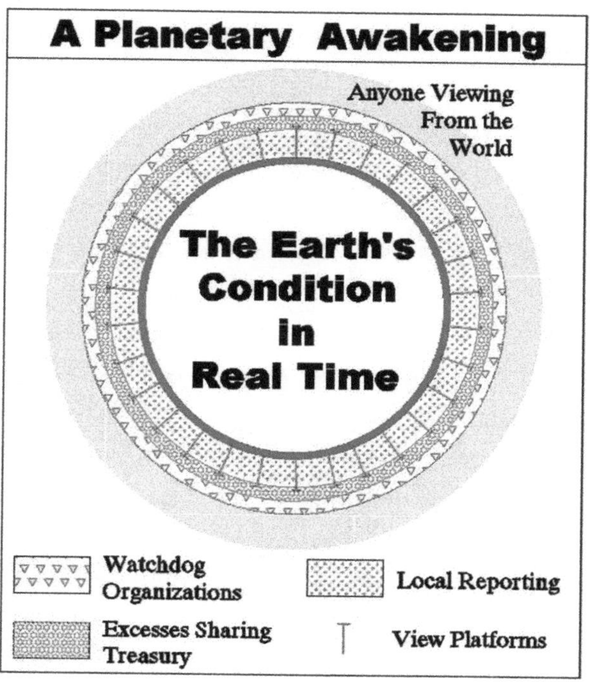

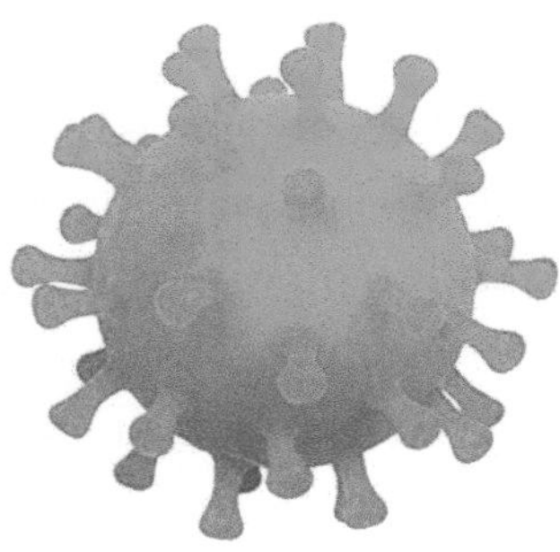

Looking at the Planetary Awakening diagram above, in 3D, it would resemble this covid stress ball but with many more spikes.

The expanding corruption watchdogs will link and form an umbrella of checks and balances around the world shown with triangle hatching, which then interact with the locally built view platforms to see the current good and bad happenings and react accordingly. The view platforms would be created and stream local reports of good deeds, corruption, environmental issues, and so on. This live-time in your living room picture can be viewed from any place on earth, right at each of our fingertips. From these view platforms, help-groups, foundations, charities, anyone, and social media advertising revenues can contribute their excesses to the sharing treasury pool for distribution as best needed. Also, individuals in crisis, as previously mentioned, can easily connect with the help-group for their specific need while new help-groups continue emerging, filling in missing areas in this free help market.

For added protection, it itself needs to be reported on for good and bad workings. Also, these systems must not become the monster itself, from which we are trying to protect ourselves. It must come from the bottom up to avoid a "Big Brother" from a top-down scenario we all fear.

Here is a close-up view of how a single platform can work:

The above "typical community platform" is only one of a locally based global network, all of which can be accessed through a global gateway, or perhaps by the place's name to see what's happening at that moment. The umbrella-sharing treasury pool network connects with all these local view platforms and would have a built-in set of criteria, ranking extreme to lesser needs in relation to the local priorities. To address these needs, the treasury pool will dispense aid relevant to the most critical social/cultural/economic/environmental needs in the entire world. It would be very much like rain coming down to bring aid to all in need.

The outer "anyone-viewing" umbrella-carrying ads will disclose our world's unabridged conditions, building empathy for sharing. The next inner umbrella would focus on cleaning up corruption, and the most inner would fulfill the needs from donated excesses and advertising revenues. Each culture could have doctors, architect, and so on come to help through this awakening; if not in person, virtually, to give knowledge or aid.

Components in the design of the view platform could include the current status of:

1. Agriculture;
2. Fresh water;
3. Economics;
4. Schools;
5. Health care;
6. Housing;
7. Family life;
8. Birth control;
9. Government structure;
10. Corruption and good deeds;
11. Priorities based on the local culture:
    a. Where the most need is required
    b. Anything important to the locals population; and
12. Feedback showing changes, hopefully improvements.

Once the view platform is designed and up for view, it will continue to change based on internal events, external aid, and contributions. Anyone viewing can choose to connect with or report to the inner layers for contributions or report corruption. However, each viewing platform can only be modified by the local people specific to that site.

Benefits from this are systems are:

1. Site is built by a locally trained IT team;
2. It is not tied to news networks, whom always chase "scoops," leaving old news for the popular news;
3. Easy and inexpensive to access from anywhere with Wi-Fi;
4. Those who are not Wi-Fi savvy or don't have internet can report in person or by mail;

5. It offers grassroots, real time interactions, no longer isolated from the rest of the world;
6. Not only a great helping tool but also an educational one;
7. Each view platform, from "outside," is a culturally appropriate reporting platform grown from "below";
8. It works for public and private deeds, good and bad;
9. View platform changes in real-time as things get worse or improve;
10. Can reflect changing human, economic, and environmental conditions; and
11. Will nurture global empathy, being easier to help when it is no longer "so far away."

<u>Contributions (Excesses) can be:</u>

1. Money;
2. Professional aid: medical, engineering, architects, education, builders, environmentalists, and so on;
3. Time/volunteering in person;
4. Arts and music; and
5. Other needs as they may arise.

<u>Local reporting will include:</u>

1. Civil heroes, both local and from the excess sharing pool;
2. Corruption activities and personnel;
3. Environmental conditions; and
4. Anything as seen important to the local people.

If this system was in place, it could have helped Madagascar in August 2021, when it was going through the worst drought in over forty years, leading to tens of thousands of people suffering in catastrophic levels of hunger.

> *"My children and I have been eating this every day now for eight months because we have nothing else to eat and no rain to allow us to harvest what we have sown," she added. "Today we have absolutely nothing to eat except cactus leaves," said Bole, a mother of three, sitting on the dry earth. She said her husband had recently died of hunger, as had a neighbour, leaving her with two more children to feed. "What can I say? Our life is all about looking for cactus leaves, again and again, to survive."* Source; *Madagascar on the brink of climate change-induced famine*, By Andrew Harding, BBC News

This new system could have given immediate aid, including the expertise to the development of a sound water management plan for future droughts. It would have brought these lives right into our homes, should we so choose, seeing the worst and then the improving social/economic situation through the impact of sharing.

This system reduces the need for news networks reporting the event. In developing countries, the news teams are often outsiders, making it difficult for reporters to get there, and with other simultaneous events, it may be easier for them to report something else. With this system, it is the locals making their own "news" with their condition, interpretation, and priorities to share with the world. Perhaps instead of cheering for your favorite sports team, it will be for some previously unknown or forgotten village on the other side of the planet.

With anything new, there are always new questions. Here are a few of them:

1. Why would anyone open this umbrella and look at any view platforms?
2. Who organizes the gathering of excesses for the treasury pool?
3. How do these excesses get redistributed?
4. How does good and bad behavior come to justice?

5. Does this redistribution stifle the individual as socialism does via third-party dependency?
6. What if the local platform is distorting the truth for false gain?
7. Will these struggling and developing locations want to be on live-stream?

Here are some answers:

1. Why would anyone open this umbrella and look at these view platforms?

   We've all seen how people like to watch others, with each of these view platforms as real-life drama horrifying, sad, and triumphant. These links can be used in schools, universities, and by the industry toward research, development, and innovation of appropriate technologies relevant to each specific situation. The global umbrella would also indicate the villains and heroes around the world. The small villains and heroes within each local view platform and larger ones on the global stage, including if the super-rich are good players or bad. Through this system, we can make bonds with local individuals, communities, their efforts, their dreams, and so on.

2. Who organizes the gathering of excesses for the treasury pool?

   Today, we see many organizations, some of which were previously listed, and there are so many more, most working independently with overlapping causes. Should a "plug in and play" world web be created, each can maintain their existing autonomy and internal structure and be better connected to the real and timely humanitarian needs around the world. Some may decide not to join, but as in any free market of business or charity, these "holes" or voids will be filled in by someone else's caring efforts and perhaps more efficiently.

3. How do these excesses get redistributed?

   First, anyone who wants to contribute needs to look at what they have versus what they can give up. Of course, money can help with almost anything, but the diversity of the other contributions is also very important. When all these excesses are placed into the treasury pool, they behave very much like things do under the invisible hand in the free market. In the free market, missing opportunities can be seen as market holes, to be filled by a new service or industry. The same can be said about needs; if something is missing (a "hole"), the appropriate resources will go there first. The global and local needs will keep changing, as will the contributions filling them, like a second emphatic invisible hand for sharing and redistributing the excess rewards from the first invisible hand.

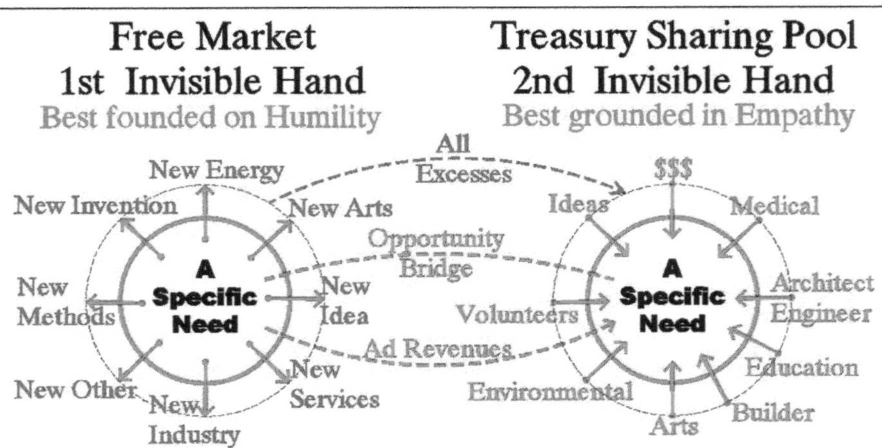

Two Invisible Hands to fill two voids.
1st hand makes excesses them shared to the 2nd hand.
What the Free-market was supposed to do from its inception.

4. How does good and bad behavior come to justice?

   The existing corruption and good deeds watchdogs would continue to grow and new ones form, focusing on public and private corruption, environmental impacts, political graft, and so on. Hopefully, they would join into this global system, overlapping with each of the local view platforms for an incredible web for justice, independent from the government and the industry, non-profit, free of partisan influence, and with a skeletal type staff and structure for maximum transparency. These watchdogs could also identify those with extreme excess who choose to turn a blind eye, leading perhaps to mandatory sharing or financial capping for those individuals/entities, as previously discussed. The exposed bad actors can be turned over to the local, state, national, or global justice system. On the other side of this, those with extreme excess choosing to contribute can be celebrated and remembered in history books as good world citizens.

5. Does this redistribution create third-party dependency as seen in socialism?

   This given aid is to provide the basic necessities for life, which most developed societies take for granted, such as clean water, sanitation, famine, disease eradication, and so on. This aid is so much deeper than someone getting regular welfare checks. Also, the priorities and needs come from the local level, and all work associated with given aid would be done by the locals, creating jobs and skill development. Money donated can be used toward infrastructure development as well as training, education, medicine, and so on.

6. What if the local platform is distorting the truth for false gain?

This is a real concern, as often the main reason for these poor conditions in struggling and developing locations is from corrupt leadership. This system is a great opportunity for the watchdog groups, linked with the local platform, to expose these tyrants to the entire world. Make the rats scurry with no place to hide and face real justice. Also, with many of these platforms up and running, there would be some overlap with neighboring villages and countries. Should one platform exaggerate conditions, it would appear as feedback anomaly, leading to further investigation of its authenticity within this awakening.

7. Will these struggling and developing locations want to be on live-stream?

   With each viewing platform being built internally, they will be tailored to their own specific level of disclosure comfort. Perhaps, initially, they would only upload essential life-and-death needs for help, but when witnessing the generosity the world has to offer, trust can be born to share their deeper treasures of their arts and culture. This will lead to a more personal relationship with the world outside of our own, one which can build the missing appreciation and empathy in our social/economics relations as human beings.

"It's unrealistic to think that the future of humanity can be achieved only on the basis of prayer; what we need is to take action." — Dalai Lama

Rather than fear, control, oppression, or government-imposed regulation . . . opportunity, freedom, cooperation, and sharing can be increased for all, specific to each of our cultures through this organic world, embracing reward and the justice-due system. It can bypass the news media for anyone to directly see and hear from the people. When the world's pain, suffering, or victory is right in front of us, we become more informed, involved, and emphatic.

> *"To practice humility and empathy, we must step outside the bounds of ourselves first, and then outside of our own little tribes. It's human nature to want to be with our own people, our kind, our squad. It's easier, often more fun, always more comfortable to spend our time with people like us. And yet, if we want to make a difference, we must approach and engage with people who think, look, and act differently. We must be willing to say to the world at large, "I recognize that I don't have all the answers." (That's humility.) "And I acknowledge that you can help me fill in those gaps." (That's empathy.) Humility is the understanding that we can't go it alone. Empathy is the ability to identify with the challenges that have brought other people to where they are. Combined, these two traits invite us into authentic relationships with others, allowing collaborative energy to begin to flow. Humility keeps us open to new information, new insights, new wisdom. Empathy encourages us to unite."* Source; Tyndale, *The Power of Humility and Empathy*, April 22, 2019

We need to remember as John Lennon said, *"The people have the power. All we have to do is awaken the power in the people."* Source: https://www.azquotes.com/quote/798840

This cultural awakening or something very much like it will come to be, and from it will emerge a much-needed global empathy through expanded disclosure of bringing our real human condition into each of our homes and businesses.

From a philosophical perspective, socialism is trust in the government, and capitalism is trust in humanity. To throw away trust in humanity because of a few bad people is illogical. It mirrors charging all of humanity for the crimes of a few. Why should all humanity be on an expensive, inefficient government leash? By trusting in humanity and remaining free, there will be cheaters, but this awakening is like a double-edged sword with one edge swift to bring them to justice, while the other simplifies our ability to cooperate and nurture a decent quality of life for all, a true balm to the dire needs around the world.

About the Author

Raymond Chladny has practiced architecture for over forty-two years with the first twenty-one years in Canada, twenty years of which were based in the Northwest Territories. Arriving in Canada's Arctic in 1981 as an active professional, the deeply embedded colonization of the indigenous people by the government was obvious and ripe for change. By flying into small Inuit and Dene communities at his own expense, Raymond began encouraging local leaders to take back control of their own villages. These efforts, along with letters of awareness to local papers, followed by government threats to be blacklisted from future work made for difficult but worthy times of transformations toward freedom in partnership with the Inuit and Dene leaders.

Trusted relationships grew, and his firm developed into a multinational, working the circumpolar, including Canada, Alaska, the Baltics, Scandinavia, Siberia, and China. Experiencing many different government systems while running a business, facing the struggles of long days, and working weekends for decades, Raymond gathered a wide perspective of how different economies work or don't work, seeing how government systems, economic structures, and societal well-being are inseparable.

Due to uncapped taxation from the Canadian government in 2001, Raymond closed his Canadian office and moved to Florida to start over again. While in Florida, Raymond met Peter Pedicini, a highly respected financial advisor to bank presidents, Florida Governor

Charlie Crist, and a colleague of Allan Greenspan. Peter's ten-year friendship and financial mentorship were transformative.

In 1997, Raymond was asked to fill a "hole" as a professor in a Toronto school of architecture for one semester. On its completion, he was offered tenure, which he declined so to continue running his business.

Raymond has given lectures about architecture, business, and ethics for success to government leaders and ambassadors of Finland, Soviet Union, Estonia, and Canada, as well as to the staff and students of several universities.

Always being fascinated by history and philosophy, combined with decades of diverse economic experiences, it has spawned many insights toward a healthy, more prosperous economic world.

Raymond's previous book, *From Superstition to Maturity, the Evolution of Religion*, is an extensive historic and philosophical study of the world's mainstream religions, connecting their history, teachings, bloodlines, and prophecies, indicating, through investigation, their commonality via interconnections over the course of millennia and a hope toward peace through knowledge transcending simple belief.

In memory of Peter Pedicini,
June 4, 1947–May 7, 2018

CPSIA information can be obtained
at www.ICGtesting.com
Printed in the USA
LVHW071706220822
726590LV00021B/613

9 781662 855184